OPPOSING
VIEWPOINTS®
SERIES

Endangered Species

Other Books of Related Interest:

Opposing Viewpoints Series

Conserving the Environment

Hunting

At Issue Series

Is Global a Threat?

"Congress shall make no law ... abridging the freedom of speech, or of the press."

First Amendment to the U.S. Constitution

The basic foundation of our democracy is the First Amendment guarantee of freedom of expression. The Opposing Viewpoints series is dedicated to the concept of this basic freedom and the idea that it is more important to practice it than to enshrine it.

Endangered Species

Viqi Wagner, Book Editor

GREENHAVEN PRESS

An imprint of Thomson Gale, a part of The Thomson Corporation

Detroit • New York • San Francisco • New Haven, Conn. • Waterville, Maine • London

Christine Nasso, *Publisher*
Elizabeth Des Chenes, *Managing Editor*

© 2008 The Gale Group.

For more information, contact:
Greenhaven Press
27500 Drake Rd.
Farmington Hills, MI 48331-3535
Or you can visit our Internet site at http://www.gale.com

LIBRARY OF CONGRESS CATALOGING-IN-PUBLICATION DATA

Endangered species / Viqi Wagner, book editor.
   p. cm. -- Opposing Viewpoints
   Includes bibliographical references and index.
   ISBN-13: 978-0-7377-2931-3 (hardcover)
   ISBN-13: 978-0-7377-2932-0 (pbk.)
   1. Endangered species--Juvenile literature. 2. Nature conservation--Juvenile literature. I. Wagner, Viqi, 1953-
   QH75.E665 2008
   333.95'22--dc22
                                                      2007038314

ISBN-10: 0-7377-2931-7 (hardcover)
ISBN-10: 0-7377-2932-5 (pbk.)

Printed in the United States of America
10 9 8 7 6 5 4 3 2 1

Contents

Why Consider Opposing Viewpoints?

> "The only way in which a human being can make some approach to knowing the whole of a subject is by hearing what can be said about it by persons of every variety of opinion and studying all modes in which it can be looked at by every character of mind. No wise man ever acquired his wisdom in any mode but this."
>
> John Stuart Mill

In our media-intensive culture it is not difficult to find differing opinions. Thousands of newspapers and magazines and dozens of radio and television talk shows resound with differing points of view. The difficulty lies in deciding which opinion to agree with and which "experts" seem the most credible. The more inundated we become with differing opinions and claims, the more essential it is to hone critical reading and thinking skills to evaluate these ideas. Opposing Viewpoints books address this problem directly by presenting stimulating debates that can be used to enhance and teach these skills. The varied opinions contained in each book examine many different aspects of a single issue. While examining these conveniently edited opposing views, readers can develop critical thinking skills such as the ability to compare and contrast authors' credibility, facts, argumentation styles, use of persuasive techniques, and other stylistic tools. In short, the Opposing Viewpoints series is an ideal way to attain the higher-level thinking and reading skills so essential in a culture of diverse and contradictory opinions.

In addition to providing a tool for critical thinking, Opposing Viewpoints books challenge readers to question their own strongly held opinions and assumptions. Most people form their opinions on the basis of upbringing, peer pressure, and personal, cultural, or professional bias. By reading carefully balanced opposing views, readers must directly confront new ideas as well as the opinions of those with whom they disagree. This is not to simplistically argue that everyone who reads opposing views will—or should—change his or her opinion. Instead, the series enhances readers' understanding of their own views by encouraging confrontation with opposing ideas. Careful examination of others' views can lead to the readers' understanding of the logical inconsistencies in their own opinions, perspective on why they hold an opinion, and the consideration of the possibility that their opinion requires further evaluation.

Evaluating Other Opinions

To ensure that this type of examination occurs, Opposing Viewpoints books present all types of opinions. Prominent spokespeople on different sides of each issue as well as well-known professionals from many disciplines challenge the reader. An additional goal of the series is to provide a forum for other, less-known, or even unpopular viewpoints. The opinion of an ordinary person who has had to make the decision to cut off life support from a terminally ill relative, for example, may be just as valuable and provide just as much insight as a medical ethicist's professional opinion. The editors have two additional purposes in including these less-known views. One, the editors encourage readers to respect others' opinions—even when not enhanced by professional credibility. It is only by reading or listening to and objectively evaluating others' ideas that one can determine whether they are worthy of consideration. Two, the inclusion of such viewpoints encourages the important critical thinking skill of objectively evaluating an author's credentials and bias. This evaluation will illuminate an author's reasons for taking a particular stance on an issue and will aid in readers' evaluation of the author's ideas.

It is our hope that these books will give readers a deeper understanding of the issues debated and an appreciation of the complexity of even seemingly simple issues when good and honest people disagree. This awareness is particularly important in a democratic society such as ours in which people enter into public debate to determine the common good. Those with whom one disagrees should not be regarded as enemies but rather as people whose views deserve careful examination and may shed light on one's own.

Thomas Jefferson once said that "difference of opinion leads to inquiry, and inquiry to truth." Jefferson, a broadly educated man, argued that "if a nation expects to be ignorant and free . . . it expects what never was and never will be." As individuals and as a nation, it is imperative that we consider the opinions of others and examine them with skill and discernment. The Opposing Viewpoints series is intended to help readers achieve this goal.

David L. Bender and Bruno Leone,
Founders

Introduction

"We are the most dangerous species of life on the planet, and every other species, even the earth itself, has cause to fear our power to exterminate. But we are also the only species which, when it chooses to do so, will go to great effort to save what it might destroy."

—Wallace Stegner

Extinction is a normal, inevitable aspect of evolution. The familiar statistic that 90 percent of all the species that ever lived on Earth are extinct reflects this principle. But the rate of extinction is not uniform. Based on a plentiful marine fossil record, paleontologists have calculated a baseline, or background, rate that anticipates the extinction of two to five taxonomic families of vertebrates and marine invertebrates every million years, also expressed as one extinction per million species per year. Several times in the past 550 million years, however, the extinction rate exceeded this background rate, and five extinction events were so massive that, in each period, 50 to 95 percent of all species on the planet died out.

There is consensus among biologists that Earth is currently experiencing a sixth mass extinction event that threatens to rival those of the geological past. Only 1.7 million of the estimated 10 to 50 million species alive today have been identified, but based on extinctions among known species and the extent of known habitat destruction, biologists calculate that the actual extinction rate is 100 to 10,000 times higher than normal, and that up to 50 percent of all species will be lost within the next century. A comparison of the previous five mass extinctions and the present-day event—known to conservation biologists in geological terms as the Holocene extinction event—yields both similarities and troubling differences.

The Five Great Mass Extinctions of Geological History

According to the fossil record, the first great extinction of species on Earth occurred roughly 444 million years ago, at the end of the Ordovician period. This 44.6-million-year period started and ended with extinction events, but it is the latter that ranks as one of the "big five." At this stage of geological history, most complex multicellular species lived in the sea—trilobites, many kinds of shell-secreting organisms, and early vertebrate fish. Scientists estimate 49 percent of genera (some 85 percent of all species) went extinct over a one- to three-million-year span.

The second major extinction event came in the Late Devonian period, about 360 million years ago. Some 70 percent of all species died in this prolonged event, mostly shallow warm-water marine organisms, and mostly invertebrates.

The Permian event, 251 million years ago, is the greatest mass extinction on Earth. According to paleontologists Jack Sepkoski and David Raup, who developed the controversial theory that mass extinctions are cyclic, occurring approximately every 26 million years, this "Great Dying" killed "96 percent of all marine species and an estimated 70 percent of land species (including plants, insects, and vertebrate animals)." But biodiversity returned: This extinction made way for dinosaurs to emerge as the dominant land vertebrates.

A fourth major extinction occurred 200 million years ago, at the end of the Triassic period, when dinosaurs and mammals first evolved. Nearly all non-dinosaur reptiles, all large amphibians, and about 20 percent of marine families were eliminated, another boost for dinosaurs, mammals, and the evolutionary branch that would become birds.

The fifth great mass extinction, 65 million years ago, is the most famous. While some taxonomic families had relatively light losses, the dinosaurs were wiped out along with 50 percent of the rest of living species. Known as the Cretaceous extinction, this event made possible the rise of mammals into the terrestrial niches once held by dinosaurs.

There is general agreement about the timing and extent of these five mass extinction events, but considerable debate about their causes—and most scientists think in terms of causes, not a single cause, that trigger such significant increases in extinction rates. In 2006, N.C. Arens and I.D. West theorized that mass extinctions "require two kinds of cause: long-term pressure on the ecosystem ('press') and a sudden catastrophe ('pulse') towards the end of the period of pressure." Widely supported "press" explanations for the big five extinction events include prolonged global cooling that caused sustained drops in sea levels and glaciation (Ice Ages), prolonged global warming that robbed the ocean of oxygen and destroyed the ozone layer, and continental drift that changed ocean and wind currents. "Pulse" explanations include volcanic eruptions, a gamma ray burst from an exploding Milky Way star, and particularly in the Cretaceous extinction, an impact event such as the collision of an asteroid or comet with Earth.

The Sixth Extinction and *Homo Sapiens*

Paleontologist Niles Eldredge of the American Museum of Natural History makes a crucial distinction between the five previous mass extinction events and the current extinction crisis: Today's global extinction event is "patently human-caused":

> There is little doubt that humans are the direct cause of ecosystem stress and species destruction in the modern world through such activities as transformation of the landscape; overexploitation of species; pollution; and the intro-

duction of alien species. And because *Homo sapiens* is clearly a species of animal ... the Sixth Extinction would seem to be the first recorded global extinction event that has a biotic, rather than a physical, cause.

Add to these "press" factors a possible "pulse" factor—the rapid warming of the planet as a result of human activity—and conditions are alarmingly like those of past mass extinction events. Certainly the "press" causes of species extinction today will only get worse if the planet continues to warm. If rising ocean levels and average temperatures drive people out of low-lying and hot regions to cooler, higher elevations, population density and pollution there will increase, habitat loss and fragmentation will be accelerated, and competition for resources will intensify. Species that cannot migrate, or whose existence depends on fixed growth cycles and ranges of temperature, are unlikely to survive, and the rate of climate change may be too rapid to allow for evolutionary adaptation.

But many scientists hold out hope that mass species extinction, with catastrophic consequences for humankind, is not yet inevitable. As Eldredge concludes:

Conservation measures, sustainable development, and ultimately stabilization of human population numbers and consumption patterns seem to offer some hope that the Sixth Extinction will not develop to the extent of the third global extinction. . . .

Though it is true that life, so incredibly resilient, has always recovered . . . after major extinction spasms, it is only after whatever has caused the extinction event has dissipated. That cause, in the case of the Sixth Extinction, is ourselves. . . . We can continue on the path to our own extinction, or, preferably, we modify our behavior toward the global ecosystem of which we are still very much a part.

The authors in *Opposing Viewpoints: Endangered Species* debate the status and future of the world's endangered species in the following chapters: Is Species Extinction a Serious Threat? Is Global Warming Endangering Plant and Animal Species? Are International Efforts to Preserve Endangered Species Effective? and How Should Humans Respond to Species Decline? The geological record underscores the pressing need for long-term solutions that serve both human needs and ecological imperatives.

CHAPTER 1

Is Species Extinction a Serious Threat?

Chapter Preface

Attenborough's long-beaked echidna of the South Pacific island of New Guinea is a spiny, egg-laying mammal that looks like a small porcupine with a long horn of a snout. It is, according to Kate Ravilious of *National Geographic News*, "so rare that no scientist has ever seen one alive." It is one of ten species labeled "evolutionarily distinct and globally endangered" (EDGE) and unofficially considered to be extinct. Until 2007, that is, when New Guinea hunters told Zoological Society of London scientists that they had seen the echidna within six miles of the nearest village and "the meat was very greasy and extremely tasty." A society expedition promptly investigated the claim, indeed identified echidna feeding holes, and pronounced the creature endangered but quite alive.

Scientists were similarly shocked in 2004 when the ivory-billed woodpecker, thought to be extinct since 1920, was sighted in the Big Woods of eastern Arkansas. It is one of a handful of species, including the New Zealand storm petrel and a Madagascar freshwater fish, called Lazarus species, back from the dead. The World Conservation Union (IUCN) happily reclassified these species on its so-called Red List, the world's most authoritative inventory of more than forty thousand known species classified by their conservation status.

How are species classified as extinct? Craig Hilton-Taylor, the British manager of the Red List, says the common assumption that a species is declared extinct when it has not been sighted for fifty years is a myth:

> It takes a long time to accumulate enough evidence before we can say, "It's extinct." . . . A detailed survey has to be carried out in the species' natural habitat, and its findings reviewed every four or five years. . . . To get a survey done in a remote area can be quite tricky and can take several years before we can finally say "It's not there anymore."

The Red List Extinct category is getting larger, slowly. It includes 784 documented extinctions (recorded since A.D. 1500; 18 additions since 2000); another 60 species are listed as Extinct in the Wild. Scientists are most concerned, however, by the large number of species entering the next-most-threatened categories, Critically Endangered (3,071 species) and Endangered (an alarming 40 percent of all organisms, extrapolated from a sample of species evaluated through 2006). The IUCN estimates the rate of movement into these categories is 100 to 1,000 times the "background" rate expected from normal evolutionary processes.

The viewpoints in this chapter debate the reasons for and meaning of current extinction rates. Meanwhile, in August 2007 another EDGE species, the Yangtze River dolphin, was officially declared extinct, representing the first large vertebrate extinction in fifty years and the only cetacean believed driven to extinction by human activity.

> "[Harvard biologist Edward O.] Wilson predicts that our present course will lead to the extinction of half of all plant and animal species by the year 2100."

Mass Species Extinction Is Imminent

Julia Whitty

Scientists have identified five cataclysmic extinction events on Earth in the past 439 million years, each wiping out 50 to 95 percent of the planet's living species. In this viewpoint, Julia Whitty warns that a sixth great extinction is occurring now, threatening human existence as well as one in four mammals, one in eight birds, one in three amphibians, 51 percent of reptiles, 52 percent of insects, and 73 percent of flowering plants. Whitty argues that humans fail to recognize species interdependence and the critical importance of biodiversity at their own peril, and she presents evidence supporting the hypothesis that human activity is accelerating species extinction beyond ecosystems' ability to recover. Nature writer and oceanic documentary producer Julia Whitty is a regular contributor to Mother Jones *magazine and the author of* Fragile Edge: Diving and Other Adventures in the South Pacific.

Julia Whitty, "Gone," *Mother Jones*, vol. 34, May–June 2007, pp. 36–45, 88. Copyright © 2007 Foundation for National Progress. Reproduced by permission.

As you read, consider the following questions:

1. What do scientists recognize as the continual, "normal" extinction rate, and how many times greater than this background rate is the current rate of species extinction, according to Whitty?

2. What causes of extinction, amplified exponentially in the twentieth century, does Whitty say are responsible for today's explosive extinction rate?

3. How does Brown and Heske's study of the Chihuahuan Desert demonstrate that removal of a very few species leads to coextinction and dramatically alters an ecosystem, according to the author?

In the final stages of dehydration the body shrinks, robbing youth from the young as the skin puckers, eyes recede into orbits, the tongue swells and cracks. Brain cells shrivel and muscles seize. The kidneys shut down. Blood volume drops, triggering hypovolemic shock, with its attendant respiratory and cardiac failures. These combined assaults disrupt the chemical and electrical pathways of the body until all systems cascade toward death.

Such is also the path of a dying species. Beyond a critical point, the collective body of a unique kind of mammal or bird or amphibian or tree cannot be salvaged, no matter the first aid rendered. Too few individuals spread too far apart or too genetically weakened are susceptible to even small natural disasters. A passing thunderstorm. An unexpected freeze. Drought. At fewer than 50 members, populations experience increasingly random fluctuations until a kind of fatal arrhythmia takes hold. Eventually, an entire genetic legacy, born in the beginnings of life on Earth, is smote from the future.

Scientists recognize that species continually disappear at a background extinction rate estimated at about one species per million species per year, with new species replacing the lost in a sustainable fashion. Occasional mass extinctions convulse this orderly norm, followed by excruciatingly slow recoveries as new species emerge from the remaining gene pool until the world is once again repopulated by a different catalog of flora and fauna. From what we understand so far, five great extinction events have reshaped Earth in cataclysmic ways in the past 439 million years, each one wiping out between 50 and 95 percent of the life of the day, including the dominant life-forms, the most recent event killing off the non-avian dinosaurs. Speciations followed, but an analysis published in *Nature* showed that it takes 10 million years before biological diversity even begins to approach what existed before a die-off.

The Sixth Great Extinction Is Now

Today we're living through the sixth great extinction, sometimes known as the Holocene extinction event. We carried its seeds with us 50,000 years ago as we migrated beyond Africa with Stone Age blades, darts, and harpoons, entering pristine Ice Age ecosystems and changing them forever by wiping out at least some of the unique mega-fauna of the times, including, perhaps, the saber-toothed cats and woolly mammoths. When the ice retreated, we terminated the long and biologically rich epoch sometimes called the Edenic period with assaults from our newest weapons: hoes, scythes, cattle, goats, pigs.

But as harmful as our forebears may have been, nothing compares to what's under way today. Throughout the 20th century the causes of extinction—habitat degradation, overexploitation, agricultural monocultures, human-borne invasive species, human-induced climate change—amplified exponentially, until now in the 21st century the rate is nothing short of explosive. The World Conservation Union's, Red List—a database measuring the global status of Earth's 1.5 million scientifically named species—tells a haunting tale of unchecked, unaddressed, and accelerating biocide.

When we hear of extinction, most of us think of the plight of the rhino, tiger, panda, or blue whale. But these sad sagas are only small pieces of the extinction puzzle. The overall numbers are terrifying. Of the 40,168 species that the 10,000 scientists in the World Conservation Union have assessed, 1 in 4 mammals, 1 in 8 birds, 1 in 3 amphibians, 1 in 3 conifers and other gymnosperms are at risk of extinction. The peril faced by other classes of organisms is less thoroughly analyzed, but fully 40 percent of the examined species of planet Earth are in danger, including up to 51 percent of reptiles, 52 percent of insects, and 73 percent of flowering plants.

By the most conservative measure—based on the last century's recorded extinctions—the current rate of extinction is 100 times the background rate. But eminent Harvard biologist Edward O. Wilson and other scientists estimate that the true rate is more like 1,000 to 10,000 times the background rate. The actual annual sum is only an educated guess, because no scientist believes the tally of life ends at the 1.5 million species already discovered; estimates range as high as 100 million species on Earth, with 10 million as the median guess. Bracketed between best- and worst-case scenarios, then, somewhere between 2.7 and 270 species are erased from existence every day. Including today.

We now understand that the majority of life on Earth has never been—and will never be—known to us. In a staggering forecast, Wilson predicts that our present course will lead to the extinction of half of all plant and animal species by the year 2100.

Mass Extinction Threatens Human Existence

You probably had no idea. Few do. A poll by the American Museum of Natural History finds that 7 in 10 biologists believe that mass extinction poses a colossal threat to human existence, a more serious environmental problem than even its contributor, global warming, and that the dangers of mass extinction are woefully underestimated by most everyone outside of science. In the 200 years since French naturalist Georges Cuvier first floated the concept of extinction, after examining fossil bones and concluding "the existence of a world previous to ours, destroyed by some sort of catastrophe," we have only slowly recognized and attempted to correct our own catastrophic behavior.

Some nations move more slowly than others. In 1992, an international summit produced a treaty called the Convention on Biological Diversity that was subsequently ratified by 190 nations—all except the unlikely coalition of the United States, Iraq, the Vatican, Somalia, Andorra, and Brunei. The European Union later called on the world to arrest the decline of species and ecosystems by 2010. Last year, worried biodiversity experts called for establishing a scientific body akin to the Intergovernmental Panel on Climate Change to provide a united voice on the extinction crisis and urge governments to action.

Yet despite these efforts, the Red List, updated every two years, continues to show metastatic growth. There are a few heartening examples of so-called Lazarus species lost and then found: the Wollemi pine and the mahogany glider in Australia, the Jerdon's courser in India, the takahe in New Zealand, and, maybe, the ivory-billed woodpecker in the United States. But for virtually all others, the Red List is a dry country with little hope of rain, as species ratchet down the listings from secure to vulnerable to endangered to critically endangered to extinct.

All these disappearing species are part of a fragile membrane of organisms wrapped around Earth so thin, writes E. O. Wilson, that it "cannot be seen edgewise from a space shuttle, yet so internally complex that most species composing it remain undiscovered." We owe everything to this membrane of life. Literally everything. The air we breathe. The food we eat. The materials of our homes, clothes, books, computers, medicines. Goods and services that we can't even imagine we'll someday need will come from species we have yet to identify. The proverbial cure for cancer. The genetic fountain of youth. Immortality. *Mortality*.

The living membrane we so recklessly destroy is existence itself.

Extinction Leads to Coextinction

Biodiversity is defined as the sum of an area's genes (the building blocks of inheritance), species (organisms that can interbreed), and ecosystems (amalgamations of species in their geological and chemical landscapes). The richer an area's biodiversity, the tougher its immune system, since biodiversity includes not only the number of species but also the number of individuals within that species, and all the inherent genetic variation—life's only army against the diseases of oblivion.

Yet it's a mistake to think that critical genetic pools exist only in the gaudy show of the coral reefs, or the cacophony of the rainforest. Although a hallmark of the desert is the sparseness of its garden, the orderly progression of plants, the understated camouflage of its animals, this is only an illusion. Turn the desert inside out and upside down and you'll discover its true nature. Escaping drought and heat, life goes underground in a tangled overexuberance of roots and burrows reminiscent of a rainforest canopy, competing for moisture, not light. Animal trails crisscross this subterranean realm in private burrows engineered, inhabited, stolen, shared, and fought over by ants, beetles, wasps, cicadas, tarantulas, spiders, lizards, snakes, mice, squirrels, rats, foxes, tortoises, badgers, and coyotes.

To survive the heat and drought . . . , desert life pioneers ingenious solutions. Coyotes dig and maintain coyote wells in arroyos, probing deep for water. White-winged doves use their bodies as canteens, drinking enough when the opportunity arises to increase their body weight by more than 15 percent.

The IUCN Red List: Inventory of the World's Threatened Species

	Number of species evaluated in 2006	Number of threatened species in 2006	Number of threatened species in 2006, as % of species evaluated
Vertebrates			
Mammals	4,856	1,093	23%
Birds	9,934	1,206	12%
Reptiles	664	341	51%
Amphibians	5,918	1,811	31%
Fishes	2,914	1,173	40%
Invertebrates			
Insects	1,192	623	52%
Molluscs	2,163	975	45%
Crustaceans	537	459	85%
Plants			
Mosses	93	80	86%
Ferns and allies	212	139	66%

TAKEN FROM: World Conservation Union, *The IUCN Red List of Threatened Species*, Summary Statistics, 2006.

Black-tailed jackrabbits tolerate internal temperatures of 111 degrees. Western box turtles store water in their oversized bladders and urinate on themselves to stay cool. Mesquite grows taproots more than 160 feet deep in search of perennial moisture.

These life-forms and their life strategies compose what we might think of as the "body" of the desert, with some species acting the role of the lungs and others the liver, the blood, the skin. The trend in scientific investigation in recent decades has been toward understanding the interconnectedness of the bodily components, i.e., the effect one species has on the others. The loss of even one species irrevocably changes the desert (or the tundra, rainforest, prairie, coastal estuary, kelp forest, coral reef, and so on) *as we know it,* just as the loss of each human being changes his or her family forever.

Nowhere is this better proven than in a 12-year study conducted in the Chihuahuan Desert by James H. Brown and Edward Heske of the University of New Mexico. When a kangaroo rat guild composed of three closely related species was removed, shrublands quickly converted to grasslands, which supported fewer annual plants, which in turn supported fewer birds. Even humble players mediate stability. So when you and I hear of [the 2007] extinction of the Yangtze River dolphin, and think, *how sad,* we're not calculating the deepest cost: that extinctions lead to co-extinctions because most every living thing on Earth supports a few symbionts and hitchhikers, while keystone species influence and support a myriad of plants and animals. Army ants, for example, are known to support 100 known species, from beetles to birds. A European study finds steep declines in honeybee diversity in the last 25 years but also significant attendant declines in plants that depend on bees for pollination—a job estimated to be worth $92 billion worldwide. Meanwhile, beekeepers in 24 American states report that up to 70 percent of their colonies have recently died off, threatening $14 billion in U.S. agriculture. And bees are only a small part of the pollinator crisis.

The Decline of Amphibians

One of the most alarming developments is the rapid decline not just of species but of higher taxa, such as the class Amphibia, the 300-million-year-old group of frogs, salamanders, newts, and toads hardy enough to have preceded and then outlived most dinosaurs. Biologists first noticed die-offs two decades ago, and since have watched as seemingly robust amphibian species vanished in as little as six months. The causes cover the spectrum of human environmental assaults, including rising ultraviolet radiation from a thinning ozone layer, increases in pollutants and pesticides, habitat loss from agriculture and urbanization, invasions of exotic species, the wildlife trade, light pollution, and fungal diseases. Sometimes stressors merge to form an unwholesome synergy; an African frog brought to the West in the 1950s for use in human pregnancy tests likely introduced a fungus deadly to native frogs. Meanwhile, a recent analysis in *Nature* estimates that in the last 20 years at least 70 species of South American frogs have gone extinct as a result of climate change.

In a 2004 analysis published in *Science*, author Lian Pin Koh and colleagues predict that an initially modest co-extinction rate will climb alarmingly as host extinctions rise in the near future. Graphed out, the forecast mirrors the rising curve of an infectious disease, with the human species acting all the parts: the pathogen, the vector, the Typhoid Mary who refuses culpability, and, ultimately, one of up to 100 million victims. . . .

Wilderness Fragmentation Hastens Extinctions

[October] in Big Bend [National Park] high desert [marks] the apex of a transient butterfly explosion. Countless millions waft across the desert like bouncing confetti. Southern dogfaces, fatal metalmarks, great purple hair-streaks, American snouts, common buckeyes. Splashes of yellow, orange, blue, purple, and metallic silver flutter by, each with characteristic flight styles: hopping, skipping, low to the ground, erratic as lightning, speedy as bullets.

Scattered among them are the strong, slow fliers with black-veined orange wings. These monarch butterflies are powering across 2,000 miles of North America en route to volcanic mountains in eastern Michoacán, Mexico. None have made this journey before, and each is at least three generations removed from an ancestor who made the reverse northward migration. Nevertheless, as many as 3 billion are homing there now with a surety the lost hiker must envy.

Crossing prairies, mountains, deserts, rivers, wetlands, and woodlands, the monarchs connect these places to each other—changing the locations they visit, being changed by them. Such transfluent energy is good for all parties involved, and satisfies a deep need of wild places. Because the truth is, wildernesses get lonely. Parks and reserves need social contact with others of their kind just as bees and kangaroo rats and people do. They may survive alone, but they do not thrive. Even preserves such as Yellowstone National Park continue to lose biodiversity despite their large size and protected status.

Until now, conservation efforts have rarely addressed this reality. The protected lands we've made so far, 102,102 sites covering 7 million square miles of earth and water, total less than 4 percent of the planet's surface. Many if not most of these isolated fragments are surrounded by hostile neighbors: farms, used-car lots, urban sprawl, clearcuts.

Segregated wildlands experience the same challenges as the dwindling members of an endangered species. Spread too far apart or too genetically weakened, they're cut off from the vital contact that renews and refreshes them, and likewise suffer debilitating arrhythmias in their demographics. Initial species losses are followed by overcrowding, then by population crashes, and insularization, with its attendant biodiversity decline.

The picture is complicated by mysterious realities: that many species will not populate a small wilderness even though it's big enough for their needs. Others will not cross the openings that fragment wilderness, particularly roads, which prove impermeable barriers to many—from beetles to bears, either because they refuse to cross or because they die trying. Fragmentation also produces a dreaded edge effect by breaching the protective skin of wilderness, disrupting microclimates, allowing pathogens, alien species, and human development inside, then sealing the edges through the scarification of weed growth.

Ten thousand feet up in Mexico's Sierra Chincua, in dense forests of *oyamel* firs, arriving monarchs seek protection under heavy evergreen boughs. For millennia, these high-altitude forests transformed monarchs into winter survivors, able to weather five months of deep freeze beneath the insulating canopy. Thanks to the seasonal sanctuary, monarchs can complete the other phase of their lives, and in doing so cinch vast areas of North America from Canada to Mexico, literally connecting the landscape one milkweed bush at a time—helping milkweed to thrive and making monarchs one of the most abundant butterflies on Earth. Species connected to the milkweed economy also prosper, including aphid-farming ants, honeybees, orioles, and moths. Although monarchs do not appear on the Red List, conservation biologists consider their migration an endangered biological phenomenon—a recognition that biodiversity also embraces large temporal and geographical scales: the migration of wildebeest in the Serengeti, caribou in Canada and Alaska, saiga in Outer Mongolia, the synchronous flowering cycles of bamboo in Asia (some at 120-year intervals), the 17- and 13-year cicada emergences in North America, and the annual travels of 1 billion individual songbirds of 120 species between Canada and the tropics.

These are nature's big shows, and they're important to biodiversity. If one phase of a biological phenomenon is disrupted, the consequences are likely to ripple farther and wider than a local species extinction. The gutting of Mexico's oyamel forests by logging, slash-and-burn agriculture, charcoal manufacture, and mismanaged ecotourism do not endanger monarchs overall, because nonmigratory populations inhabit the tropics. Yet the squandering of the forests is a threat to the milkweed trading route, and thereby to the body of North America.

The fragmentation of the Sierra Chincua woodlands is already disrupting the microclimates the migrating butterflies need to survive. At the present rate of deforestation, there'll come a winter night not far in the future when a surge of cold air sinking down from Canada will overwhelm the threadbare forests, scattered too thinly to blanket the butterflies. The only monarchs that know the way north, trapped at 10,000 feet in lonely fragments of wilderness, will die. . . .

Whooping Cranes:
A Classic Example of Species Decline

Along Interstate 10 in Arizona, I happen to see a flock of big birds lumbering on the reluctant elevator of an early morning thermal—white birds with black flight feathers, afloat with outstretched necks and trailing legs, flapping with a characteristic flick on the upbeat, yodeling. They're whooping cranes, 30 adults and juveniles rearranging themselves into a lopsided V and heading west.

It's a remarkable sight since it represents about 6 percent of the total world population of whoopers. It's also a confusing sight, since at this time of year they should be well east of here en route from Canada to the Texas Gulf Coast . . . though one of the things I've learned from decades of working with animals in the wild is their ability, with the flip of a wing, to rewrite expectation. But, most of all, it's a poignant sight, these 30 whoopers, the descendants of a breeding population of only 16 birds in 1941. "Because it is a wild, wary, wilderness bird," wrote John K. Terres, longtime editor of *Audubon* magazine, "it could not stand the intrusion of mankind."

Their decline is an extinction textbook. They suffered the conversion of prairies and wetlands to farms. They were hunted for meat. By 1922, the last known breeding pair in Saskatchewan died, leaving only one winter population in Texas whose summer nesting grounds remained an intractable mystery for most of the 20th century. In 1954, the colony was finally tracked to remote Wood Buffalo National Park in Canada's Northwest Territories, about as far as they could get from human beings without leaving planet Earth.

Since then, the cranes have been rehabilitated in every way we know, as well as in ways we've made up as we went along, forging techniques now considered the blueprint for endangered species recovery. Yet whoopers today number about 500 birds: 350 in the wild, the rest in captivity. They're only marginally less vulnerable than they were in 1941. A bird flu, an oil spill, a hurricane. Seventeen died in the tornadoes that struck Florida in February [2007], highlighting how tenuously this tribe survives.

"There are at least 100 success stories among the more than 1,800 species now listed as threatened and endangered in the United States."

Hundreds of Endangered Species Are on the Road to Recovery

Environment News Service

In this viewpoint, the independent daily newswire Environment News Service (ENS) highlights conservation success stories to show that many once-endangered species have not only been saved from extinction but are thriving in the United States. Species on the road to recovery include "key deer and green sea turtles in Florida, grizzly bears and wolves in Montana, sea otters and blue butterflies in California, and short-nose sturgeon and roseate terns in New York"—the ENS credits the Endangered Species Act of 1973 and dedicated conservation groups for this turnaround. ENS, founded in 1990 by editors Sunny Lewis and Jim Crabtree and based in Washington, D.C., and Honolulu, is a network of national and international correspondents who cover science and technology, land use, wildlife and marine life, renewable energy, legislation and politics, and other issues related to the environment.

As you read, consider the following questions:

1. How would the bald eagle's recovery be assured even if the species is removed from the endangered list, according to the ENS?

2. What were the whooping crane's numbers at their low in 1941, in 1967, and in 2003, as reported by the ENS?

3. According to whale scientist Dave Rugh, quoted by the author, how is a decline in gray whale numbers since 1998 a sign of the species' health, not its endangerment?

The U.S. Senate has declared May 11 to be Endangered Species Day. The resolution, passed unanimously on April 5 [2006], states that the purpose of the Day is to "encourage the people of the United States to become educated about, and aware of, threats to species, success stories in species recovery, and the opportunity to promote species conservation worldwide."

"California's conservation efforts have already helped restore California condor, winter run chinook salmon, and California gray whale populations," said Senator Dianne Feinstein of California, a Democrat, who introduced the legislation. "But more still needs to be done, and I hope that Endangered Species Day will spark wonder and interest in conservation efforts throughout the country."

There are at least 100 success stories among the more than 1,800 species now listed as threatened and endangered in the United States. To bring these conservation successes into the spotlight, the Center for Biological Diversity has created a website detailing the efforts [that] reversed the decline of these 100 endangered species in every U.S. state and territory.

Kieran Suckling, policy director of the Center for Biological Diversity, calls the Endangered Species Act [ESA] "one of America's most successful conservation laws."

"From key deer and green sea turtles in Florida, to grizzly bears and wolves in Montana, sea otters and blue butterflies in California, and short-nose sturgeon and roseate terns in New York, the Endangered Species Act has not only saved hundreds of species from extinction," said [Suckling] "but [has] put them on the road to recovery."

Is the Endangered Species Act Too Restrictive?

The positive focus on the conservation successes of the Endangered Species Act is an answer to the legislative attempt of Congressman Richard Pombo of California to revise the 1973 law to create bigger roles for state and local governments, protect private property owners, and eliminate critical habitat designations.

Pombo, a Republican who chairs the House Resources Committee, authored a bill that passed the House in September [2005] to revise the Endangered Species Act. Pombo and the bill's cosponsor, California Congressman Dennis Cardoza, a Democrat, believe the Endangered Species Act is increasingly driven by litigation, not science, and has become a burden on local economies and landowners.

Pombo said in September that when their property is "taken" to protect endangered species, landowners must be compensated, "as the Fifth Amendment of the Constitution requires."

"Upholding this right and partnering with the landowner is the only way we are going to improve the ESA's failing results for recovery," Pombo said.

Success Stories

Conservationists support the act in its present form and point out the successes rather than the failures.

Whooping Cranes Are Thriving

The whooping crane, the tallest bird in North America, whose numbers dwindled to fewer than 20 in 1941, is not only back from the brink of extinction but also thriving—a comeback story, federal wildlife officials say, that illustrates how a coordinated conservation effort can save a species.

"The whooping crane continues to mirror the success of endangered species recovery when man sets his mind to it," said Tom Stehn, the national whooping crane coordinator for the U.S. Fish and Wildlife Service. "We have come a long way, but we do have a long, long way to go."

[In 2006], the nation's only natural wild population of whooping cranes reached a milestone. Stehn's mid-December census of the migratory crane flock at the wildlife refuge, where he is based, numbered 237. Combined with the number of birds in captivity in three special flocks raised for reintroduction to the wild and those in zoos, the crane population now numbers 518. This is the first time in more than a century that whooping cranes have numbered more than 500.

Sylvia Moreno, "After Long Struggle, Whooping Crane Population Hits Milestone," Washington Post, December 26, 2006, p. A03.

The Endangered Species Act's best known successes include the U.S. national symbol, the bald eagle. Numbers increased from 417 pairs in 1963 to 9,250 pairs in 2006.

Saying the species is healthy now, the U.S. Fish and Wildlife Service is acting on a 1999 proposal to remove the bald eagle from Endangered Species Act protection.

Once delisted from the Endangered Species Act, bald eagles will continue to be protected by the Bald and Golden Eagle Protection Act and the Migratory Bird Treaty Act. Both acts prohibit killing, selling or otherwise harming eagles, their nests or eggs. . . .

The Center for Biological Diversity points to the story of the whooping crane as another success of the Endangered Species Act. Whooping crane numbers have increased from 54 birds in 1967 to 436 in 2003.

Fossilized remains of the whooping crane date back several million years. Once the large migratory birds inhabited an area from central Canada to Mexico, and from Utah to the Atlantic coast. The species range shrank rapidly after 1850, and breeding birds were extirpated in the United States, except in Louisiana, by the 1890s. Whooping cranes in Louisiana last nested in 1939 and disappeared by 1950.

The International Crane Foundation says the only remaining natural, self-sustaining flock of whooping cranes breeds in Wood Buffalo National Park in the Northwest Territories, Canada, and winters in Aransas National Wildlife Refuge in Texas. This natural flock reached a low of only 16 birds in the winter of 1941–1942, and numbered under 35 birds over the next two decades. Conservation efforts have increased this flock to almost 200 birds in 2003. A second flock was created by humans in 1993 in case disaster wiped out the natural flock.

Recovery of Species Includes Habitat Restoration

The story of a songbird known as the Kirtland's warbler is also a success, due to cooperation among the Michigan Department of Natural Resources (DNR), the U.S. Forest Service, the U.S. Fish and Wildlife Service, and the Michigan Department of Military Affairs in restoring the warblers' nesting habitat.

Numbers of Kirtland's warblers have increased from 210 pairs of birds in 1971 to 1,415 pairs in 2005, according to the DNR.

The Kirtland's warbler population depends on northern Michigan's jack pine barrens ecosystem for nesting habitat.

The warbler nests on the ground and selects nesting sites in stands of jack pine between four and 20 years old.

These stands of young jack pine once were created by natural wildfires that frequently swept through northern Michigan. Modern fire suppression programs have altered this natural process, reducing Kirtland's warbler habitat.

To mimic the effects of wildfire and ensure the future of this endangered species, state and federal wildlife biologists and foresters annually manage the forests through a combination of clearcutting, burning, seeding and replanting to promote warbler habitat.

"Additional new habitat will become available each year for the next several years, so we believe the warbler populations will remain stable or increase," said Elaine Carlson, DNR wildlife biologist. "The success of the Kirtland's warbler management program shows that scientific wildlife management works."

Mammal Comebacks

While birds have benefited from conservation efforts under the Endangered Species Act, mammals have as well.

Eastern North Pacific gray whales counted off the U.S. Pacific coast increased from 13,095 whales in 1968 to 26,635 whales in 1998, but have declined since then, according to researchers at the National Marine Mammal Laboratory (NMML).

A census in 2002 estimated 17,414 gray whales. This is below the estimate of 18,761 whales made during the 2000–01 count and well below the 1998 estimate.

NMML whale scientist Dave Rugh wrote that abundance may have declined following high mortality rates observed in 1999 and 2000, "probably a function of this population reaching its carrying capacity."

During their annual migration along the coast, the gray whales pass through U.S. oil and gas exploration and development areas, shipping lanes, military test ranges and near coastal cities, from which whalewatchers embark.

The Center for Biological Diversity counts the grizzly bear as another Endangered Species Act success story. Grizzly numbers in the Yellowstone area increased from about 271 in 1975 to over 580 bears in 2005.

Once numbering at least 50,000, grizzly bears roamed the West, but just 136 individuals were still alive when the species was listed in 1975, according to the U.S. Fish and Wildlife Service

The bears' survival was jeopardized by loss of habitat and high mortality from conflict with humans.

In November [2005] Interior Secretary Norton proposed to remove the greater Yellowstone population of grizzly bears from the Endangered Species List.

The Fish and Wildlife Service plan calls for returning grizzly bear management in the Yellowstone area to the governments of Montana, Wyoming and Idaho.

Environmentalists say the population has recovered somewhat but not enough. Some groups, such as the Natural Resources Defense Council, warn that the states of Wyoming, Montana and Idaho all have plans to allow grizzly hunting when the bears are delisted.

Recovery of the Gray Wolf

Gray wolf populations have increased in the Northern Rockies, Southwest, and Great Lakes until now, [and] delisting proposals are in process for several of these populations.

Interior Secretary Gale Norton announced March 16 [2006], that gray wolves in Minnesota, Wisconsin and Michigan have recovered from the threat of extinction, prompting the U.S. Fish and Wildlife Service to propose removing the wolves in this region from the federal list of threatened and endangered species.

The gray wolf population in the western Great Lakes region now numbers close to 4,000 animals over the three-state area. The Minnesota population has steadily expanded, Norton said. The latest estimate in 2003–2004 found about 3,020 animals.

Wolves have become well-established in Michigan, which has 405 animals now, and in Wisconsin where 425 wolves are found. Wolf numbers in those two states combined have exceeded 100 for the past 12 years, meeting the population criteria identified in the federal recovery plans. . . .

In a separate action, the Service has announced its intention to propose delisting gray wolves in the Northern Rocky Mountains.

Delisting proposals do not affect gray wolves in the Southwest, nor do they affect red wolves, a separate species found in the Southeast.

"This first-ever Endangered Species Day gives us a chance to celebrate America's commitment to protecting our unique wildlife," said Sarah Matsumoto of the Endangered Species Coalition. "Endangered Species Day is a great opportunity for young and old alike to learn about our nation's wildlife and get involved in protecting endangered species and their habitat."

"[B]iodiversity loss ... [contributes] to worsening health, higher food insecurity, increasing vulnerability, lower material wealth, ... and less freedom for choice and action."

Mass Species Extinction Will Have Disastrous Consequences for Humankind

Millennium Ecosystem Assessment

The Millennium Ecosystem Assessment (MA) (2001–2005) is an international project conducted by more than 1,350 natural and social scientists from 95 countries (with peer review by 600 additional experts) who assessed the conditions and trends of the world's ecosystems and their effects on human well-being. To date, the MA represents the best scientific description of ecosystem change due to human activities. A major conclusion of the study is that 60 percent of assessed ecosystems are suffering loss of biodiversity—declines, often irreversible, in the number and variety of living organisms. In this viewpoint, the MA argues with "high certainty" that biodiversity loss hurts humans— pushing people into poverty, jeopardizing food supplies and hu-

Millennium Ecosystem Assessment, from *Ecosystems and Human Well-Being: Biodiversity Synthesis*. Washington, DC: World Resources Institute, 2005. Copyright © 2005 World Resources Institute. All rights reserved. Reproduced by permission.

man health, and increasing human suffering and insecurity, especially among the world's poorest populations.

As you read, consider the following questions:

1. How does biodiversity loss make humans more vulnerable to natural disasters, according to the MA?
2. What percentage of the world's labor force does the MA state depends on agriculture (which in turn depends on biodiversity) for its livelihood?
3. Who is hit hardest by biodiversity loss, and why, in the assessment of the MA?

The MA [Millennium Ecosystem Assessment] identifies biodiversity and the many ecosystem services that it provides as a key instrumental and constitutive factor determining human well-being. The MA findings support, with *high certainty*, that biodiversity loss and deteriorating ecosystem services contribute—directly or indirectly—to worsening health, higher food insecurity, increasing vulnerability, lower material wealth, worsening social relations, and less freedom for choice and action.

Food Security

Biological diversity is used by many rural communities directly as an insurance and coping mechanism to increase flexibility and spread or reduce risk in the face of increasing uncertainty, shocks, and surprises. ...

Coping mechanisms based on indigenous plants are particularly important for the most vulnerable people, who have little access to formal employment, land, or market opportunities. For example, investigations of two dryland sites in Kenya and Tanzania report local communities using wild indigenous plants to provide alternative sources of food when harvests failed or when sudden expenses had to be met (such as a hospital bill).

Another pathway through which biodiversity can improve food security is the adoption of farming practices that maintain and make use of agricultural biodiversity. Biodiversity is important to maintaining agricultural production. Wild relatives of domestic crops provide genetic variability that can be crucial for overcoming outbreaks of pests and pathogens and new environmental stresses. Many agricultural communities consider increased local diversity a critical factor for the long-term productivity and viability of their agricultural systems. For example, interweaving multiple varieties of rice in the same paddy has been shown to increase productivity by lowering the loss from pests and pathogens.

Vulnerability

The world is experiencing an increase in human suffering and economic losses from natural disasters over the past several decades. Mangrove forests and coral reefs—a rich source of biodiversity—are excellent natural buffers against floods and storms. Their loss or reduction in coverage has increased the severity of flooding on coastal communities. Floods affect more people (140 million per year on average) than all other natural or technological disasters put together. Over the past four decades, the number of "great" disasters has increased by a factor of four, while economic losses have increased by a factor of ten. During the 1990s, countries low on the Human Development Index [a standard measure of life expectancy and well-being used by the United Nations in countries] experienced about 20% of the hazard events and reported over 50% of the deaths and just 5% of economic losses. Those with high rankings on the index accounted for over 50% of the total economic losses and less than 2% of the deaths.

A common finding from the various sub-global assessments was that many people living in rural areas cherish and promote ecosystem variability and diversity as a risk management strategy against shocks and surprises.

They maintain a diversity of ecosystem services and are skeptical about solutions that reduce their options. The sub-global assessments found that diversity of species, food, and landscapes serve as "savings banks" that rural communities use to cope with change and ensure sustainable livelihoods.

Health

An important component of health is a balanced diet. About 7,000 species of plants and several hundred species of animals have been used for human food consumption at one time or another. Some indigenous and traditional communities currently consume 200 or more species. Wild sources of food remain particularly important for the poor and landless to provide a somewhat balanced diet. Overexploitation of marine fisheries worldwide, and of bushmeat in many areas of the tropics, has led to a reduction in the availability of wild-caught animal protein, with serious consequences in many countries for human health.

Human health, particularly risk of exposure to many infectious diseases, may depend on the maintenance of biodiversity in natural ecosystems. On the one hand, a greater diversity of wildlife species might be expected to sustain a greater diversity of pathogens that can infect humans. However, evidence is accumulating that greater wildlife diversity may decrease the spread of many wildlife pathogens to humans. The spread of Lyme disease, the best-studied case, seems to be decreased by the maintenance of the biotic integrity of natural ecosystems.

Energy Security

Wood fuel provides more than half the energy used in developing countries. Even in industrial countries such as Sweden and the United States, wood supplies 17% and 3% of total energy consumption, respectively. In some African countries such as Tanzania, Uganda, and Rwanda, wood fuel accounts

Marine Biodiversity Loss Threatens Human Well-Being

In a study published in the November 3, 2006, issue of the journal *Science,* an international group of ecologists and economists show that the loss of biodiversity is profoundly reducing the ocean's ability to produce seafood, resist diseases, filter pollutants, and rebound from stresses such as overfishing and climate change. The study ... reveals that every species lost causes a faster unraveling of the overall ecosystem. Conversely, every species recovered adds significantly to the overall productivity and stability of the ecosystem and its ability to withstand stresses. ...

"Marine ecosystems are like machines that have evolved to work with all of their pieces, that is, species. If they lose some of these pieces, the system may malfunction, with consequences for humans as well. Who would board a plane that has missing parts, even if they do not know what these parts are for?" said [Enric] Sala, deputy director of the Center for Marine Biodiversity and Conservation at Scripps [Institution of Oceanography at UC San Diego]. ...

The impacts of species loss go beyond declines in seafood. Human health risks emerge as depleted coastal ecosystems become vulnerable to invasive species, disease outbreaks, and noxious algal blooms. ...

Scripps Institution of Oceanography,
"Accelerating Loss of Ocean Species Threatens Human Well-Being,"
Scripps Oceanography News, *November 2, 2006.*
http://scrippsnews.ucsd.edu.

for 80% of total energy consumption. In rural areas, 95% is consumed in the form of firewood, while in urban areas 85% is in the form of charcoal. Shortage of wood fuel occurs in areas with high population density without access to alternative and affordable energy sources. In some provinces of Zambia where population densities exceed the national average of 13.7 persons per square kilometer, the demand for wood has already surpassed local supply. In such areas, people are vulnerable to illness and malnutrition because of the lack of resources to heat homes, cook food, and boil water. Women and children in rural poor communities are the ones most affected by wood fuel scarcity. They must walk long distances searching for firewood and therefore have less time for tending crops and school.

Provision of Clean Water

The continued loss of cloud forests and the destruction of watersheds reduce the quality and availability of water supplied to household use and agriculture. The availability of clean drinking water is a concern in dozens of the world's largest cities.

In one of the best documented cases, New York City took steps to protect the integrity of watersheds in the Catskills to ensure continued provision of clean drinking water to 9 million people. Protecting the ecosystem was shown to be far more cost-effective than building and operating a water filtration plant. New York City avoided $6–8 billion in expenses by protecting its watersheds.

Social Relations

Many cultures attach spiritual and religious values to ecosystems or their components, such as a tree, hill, river, or grove. Thus, loss or damage to these components can harm social relations—for example, by impeding religious and social ceremonies that normally bind people. Damage to ecosystems highly valued for their aesthetic, recreational, or spiritual values can damage social relations, both by reducing the bonding value of shared experience as well as by causing resentment toward groups that profit from their damage.

Freedom of Choice and Action

Freedom of choice and action within the MA context refers to individuals having control over what happens and being able to achieve what they value. Loss of biodiversity often means a loss of choices. Local fishers depend on mangroves as breeding grounds for local fish populations. Loss of mangroves translates to a loss in control over the local fish stock and a livelihood they have been pursuing for many generations and that they value. Another example is high-diversity agricultural systems. These systems normally produce less cash than monoculture cash crops, but farmers have some control over their entitlements because of spreading risk through diversity. High diversity of genotypes, populations, species, functional types, and spatial patches decreases the negative effects of pests and pathogens on crops and keeps open possibilities for agrarian communities to develop crops suited to future environmental challenges and to increase their resilience to climate variability and market fluctuations.

Another dimension of choices relates to the future. The loss of biodiversity in some instances is irreversible, and the value individuals place on keeping biodiversity for future generations—the option value—can be significant. The notion of having choices available irrespective of whether any of them will be actually picked is an essential constituent of the freedom aspect of well-being. However, putting a monetary figure on option values is notoriously difficult. We can only postulate on the needs and desires of future generations, some of which can be very different from today's aspirations.

Basic Materials for a Good Life and Sustainable Livelihoods

Biodiversity offers directly the various goods—often plants, animals, and fungi—that individuals need in order to earn an income and secure sustainable livelihoods. In addition, it also contributes to livelihoods through the support it provides for ecosystem services: The agricultural labor force currently contains approximately 22% of the world's population and accounts for 46% of its total labor force. For example, apples are a major cash crop in the Himalayan region in India, accounting for 60–80% of total household income. The region is also rich in honeybee diversity, which played a significant role in pollinating field crops and wild plants, thereby increasing productivity and sustaining ecosystem functions. In the early 1980s, market demand for particular types of apples led farmers to uproot pollinated varieties and plant new, sterile cultivars. The pollinator populations were also negatively affected by excessive use of pesticides. The result was a reduction in overall apple productivity and the extinction of many natural pollinator species.

Nature-based tourism ("ecotourism")—one of the fastest-growing segments of tourism worldwide—is a particularly important economic sector in a number of countries and a potential income source for many rural communities. The aggregate revenue generated by nature-based tourism in southern Africa was estimated to be $3.6 billion in 2000, roughly 50% of total tourism revenue. Botswana, Kenya, Namibia, South Africa, Tanzania, Uganda, and Zimbabwe each generated over $100 million in revenue annually from nature-based tourism in 2000. In Tanzania, tourism contributed 30% of the total GDP [gross domestic product] of the country.

Biodiversity also contributes to a range of other industries, including pharmaceuticals, cosmetics, and horticulture. Market trends vary widely according to the industry and country involved, but many bioprospecting activities and revenues are expected to increase over the next decades. The current economic climate suggests that pharmaceutical bioprospecting will increase, especially as new methods use evolutionary and ecological knowledge.

Losses of biodiversity can impose substantial costs on local and national scales. For example, the collapse of the Newfoundland cod fishery in the early 1990s cost tens of thousands of jobs, as well as at least $2 billion in income support and retraining. Recent evidence suggests that the preservation of the integrity of local biological communities, both in terms of the identity and the number of species, is important for the maintenance of plant and animal productivity, soil fertility, and their stability in the face of a changing environment. Recent estimates from the MA Portugal sub-global assessment indicate that environmental expenses in that country are increasing at a rate of 3% a year and are presently 0.7% of GDP. . . .

The Distributional Impacts of Biodiversity Loss and Ecosystem Change

Biodiversity use, change, and loss have improved well-being for many social groups and individuals. But people with low resilience to ecosystem changes—mainly the disadvantaged—have been the biggest losers and have witnessed the biggest increase in not only monetary poverty but also relative, temporary poverty and the depths of poverty. . . .

One of the main reasons some countries, social groups, or individuals—especially the disadvantaged—are more severely affected by biodiversity and ecosystem changes is limited access to substitutes or alternatives. When the quality of water deteriorates, the rich have the resources to buy personal water filters or imported bottled water that the poor can ill afford. Similarly, urban populations in developing countries have easier access to clean energy sources because of easy access to the electrical grid, while rural communities have fewer choices. Poor farmers often do not have the option of substituting modern methods for services provided by biodiversity because they cannot afford the alternatives. And, substitution of some services may not be sustainable, and may have negative environmental and human health effects. For example, the reliance on toxic and persistent pesticides to control certain pests can

have negative effects on the provision of services by the cultivated system and other ecosystems connected to the cultivated
system. Many industrial countries maintain seed banks in response to the rapid rate of loss of crop genetic diversity and
to make existing genetic diversity more readily available to
plant breeders. Apart from the network of seed banks maintained in developing countries by the Consultative Group on
International Agricultural Research, for many developing
countries creating such banks could pose a problem when
electricity supplies are unreliable, fuel is costly, and there is a
lack of human capacity.

> "[M]uch of the biodiversity crisis is over. People won: native plants and animals lost."

Humans Can Withstand Biodiversity Loss

Martin Jenkins

Martin Jenkins, senior advisor on species conservation for the United Nations Environment Programme's World Conservation Monitoring Centre in Cambridge, England, does not dispute current scientific measures and predictions of significant global biodiversity loss. In this viewpoint, however, Jenkins argues that humanity will cope with and adapt to species extinction and climate change, especially in developed countries in temperate zones. In fact, he says, humans benefit far more from highly productive, intensively managed, low-diversity ecosystems than from "intact" wild systems. Moreover, he contends that areas where humans are known to have directly or indirectly played a role in species extinction over the past 40,000 to 50,000 years continue to function with few signs of crisis.

As you read, consider the following questions:

1. What three conditions must hold for Jenkins's forecast to be plausible?

Martin Jenkins, "Prospects for Biodiversity," *Science*, vol. 302, November 14, 2003, pp. 1175–1177. Copyright © 2003 by AAAS. Reproduced by permission.

2. How does New Zealand's record of flightless bird extinction support Jenkins's claim that species extinction is not ecologically catastrophic?

3. According to the author, what kind of activity or event *would* likely have devastating consequences for humankind?

What will be the state of the world's biodiversity in 2050, and what goods and services can we hope to derive from it? First, some assumptions: that the United Nations median population estimate for 2050 holds, so that Earth will have roughly nine billion people—just under half again as many as are currently alive; that the Intergovernmental Panel on Climate Change scenarios provide a good indication of global average surface temperatures and atmospheric CO_2 concentrations at that time, with the former $\sim1°C$ to 2°C and the latter ~100 to 200 parts per million higher than today; and, perhaps most important, although most nebulous, that humanity as a whole has not determined on a radically new way of conducting its affairs. Here, then, is a plausible future.

In this future, the factors that are most directly implicated in changes in biodiversity—habitat conversion, exploitation of wild resources, and the impacts of introduced species—will continue to exert major influences, although their relative importance will vary regionally and across biomes. In combination, they will ensure continuing global biodiversity loss, as expressed through declines in populations of wild species and reduction in area of wild habitats.

Extinction Rates

To start, as it were, at the end: with extinction, perhaps the most tangible measure of biodiversity loss. The uncertainties that still surround our knowledge of tropical biotas (which include the great majority of extant species), the difficulty of recording extinctions, and our ability when we put our minds to it, to bring species back from the brink make it extremely difficult to assess current global extinction rates, let alone estimate future ones. However, an assessment of extinction risk in birds carried out by BirdLife International—using the criteria of IUCN—The World Conservation Union's Red List of Threatened Species—has concluded (with many caveats) that perhaps 350 species (3.5% of the world's current avifauna) might be expected to become extinct between now and 2050. Indications are that some other groups—mammals and freshwater fishes, for example—have a higher proportion of species at risk of extinction, although data for these are less complete.

Just as it is hard to estimate future extinction rates, so is it difficult to extrapolate forward from current rates of habitat alteration, even where these are known. However, some general patterns are clear. With the harvest of marine resources now at or past its peak, terrestrial ecosystems will bear most of the burden of having to feed, clothe, and house the expanded human population. This extra burden will fall most heavily on developing countries in the tropics, where the great majority of the world's terrestrial biological diversity is found.

The Land

Most increased agricultural production is expected to be derived from intensification. However, the Food and Agriculture Organization (FAO) of the United Nations notes that, on the basis of reasonably optimistic assumptions about increasing productivity, at least an extra 120 million ha [297 million acres] of agricultural land will still be needed in developing countries by 2030. In a less than wholly efficient world, the amount converted will be much more. Historic precedent and present land availability indicate that almost all new conversion will be in South America and sub-Saharan Africa. More than half the unused suitable cropland is found in just seven countries in these regions: Angola, Argentina, Bolivia, Brazil, Colombia, Democratic Republic of Congo, and Sudan. Five of these are among the 25 most biodiverse countries; the exceptions (Angola and Sudan) are both also highly biodiverse. Large-scale conversion will continue in most or all of these, with a disproportionately high impact on global biodiversity.

Much conversion here and elsewhere will be of land currently under tropical forest. Fragmentation and loss of such forests will thus continue, albeit overall possibly at a slower rate than at present. The great, largely contiguous forest blocks of Amazonia and the Zaire basin will by 2050 be a thing of the past, with unknown (and hotly debated) impacts on regional weather patterns and global climate. Deforestation pressure will remain high in the immediate future in a number of other tropical developing countries, including those such as Indonesia, Madagascar, and the Philipppines, which hold many endemic forest-dependent species, often with small ranges. Forest loss here will also have a particularly high impact on biodiversity.

There will, however, still be considerable forest cover in the tropics, much of it in inaccessible or steeply sloping sites unsuitable for clearance and in some protected areas. Even outside such areas, forest cover will be increasing in some regions, paralleling the current situation in Northern hemisphere temperate forests, because growing urbanization will lead to the abandonment of marginally productive lands, allowing reversion to a more natural state. However, uncontrolled and frequent fires will mean that abandoned lands in many areas will remain relatively degraded. In addition, almost all wild lands in the tropics will be impoverished in numbers and diversity of larger animal species, thanks to persistent overexploitation of wild resources such as bush-meat. Although there have been some local successes, the goal of large-scale sustainable harvest of these resources has so far been elusive and will remain so. This means that populations of many species will survive largely or exclusively in heavily managed protected areas.

Life Is Resilient

The natural consequence of species extinction and ecosystem destruction had been the arrival of increased biodiversity—humans included. Life is resilient. As [A. J.] van Loon explains, "[M]ass extinction never posed a threat to life itself," even during the Permian (about 290 million to 250 million years ago) and Triassic extinction episodes, in which 95% of marine life was killed and 70% of land [life] became extinct. In fact, he writes, that [the] Permian-Triassic event "allowed not only sufficient individuals to survive, but also sufficient taxa to build complex new ecosystems in which numerous new species could develop to fill up the niches that had been created by the mass extinction."

In other words, it is the natural reality of extinction events and species evolution that has led to the ultimate enrichment of ecosystems and biodiversity with niches and opportunities for new species.

"It is an interesting thought," van Loon reflects soberly, "that modern man, *Homo sapiens*, would most probably not have developed if there had not been a mass extinction at the Cretaceous/Tertiary boundary that created apparently optimum conditions for the further evolution of mammals. This should make man much more humble than he is, and make him more reluctant than he is with respect to his present-day efforts to influence the evolutionary processes."

World Climate Report, *"Disappearing Act,"* May 24, 2004.
www.worldclimatereport.com.

Although tropical developing countries will continue to suffer quite possibly accelerating biodiversity loss, much less change can be expected in developed temperate countries. Temperate forest cover will continue to increase, or at least stabilize, and many forest species will thrive, although with changes in distribution and relative abundance as a result of climate change. The recent declines in many wild species that are primarily associated with agricultural land may or may not continue. Much will depend on whether the current consumer-led drive to "greener" forms of agriculture has a major long-term impact.

Aquatic Ecosystems

Our most direct and pervasive impact on marine ecosystems and marine biodiversity is through fishing. If present trends continue, the world's marine ecosystems in 2050 will look very different from today's. Large species, and particularly top predators, will be by and large extremely scarce, and some will have disappeared entirely, giving the lie to the old assertion that marine organisms are peculiarly resistant to extinction. Marine ecosystems, particularly coastal ones, will also continue to contend with a wide range of other pressures, including siltation and eutrophication from land runoff, coastal development, conversion for aquaculture, and impacts of climate change. Areas of anoxia will increase; most coral reefs will be heavily degraded, but some adaptable species may benefit from warming and may even have started to expand in range.

Available information suggests that freshwater biodiversity has declined as a whole faster than either terrestrial or marine biodiversity over the past 30 years. The increasing demands that will be placed on freshwater resources in most parts of the world mean that this uneven loss of biodiversity will continue. Pollution, siltation, canalization, water abstraction, dam construction, overfishing, and introduced species will all play a part, although their individual impacts will vary regionally. The greatest effects will be on biodiversity in fresh waters in densely populated parts of the tropics, particularly South and Southeast Asia, and in dryland areas, although large-scale hydroengineering projects proposed elsewhere could also have catastrophic impacts. Although water quality may stabilize or improve in many inland water systems in developed countries, other factors, such as introduced species, will continue to have an adverse impact on biodiversity in most areas.

How Much Does It Matter?

In assessing the importance of environmental change, we must distinguish between wholesale degradation, such as reduction of a productive, forested slope to bedrock, and reduction in biodiversity per se through the loss of particular populations or species of wild organisms or the replacement of diverse, species-rich systems with less diverse, often intensively managed systems of nonnative species. The former can, of course, have devastating direct consequences for human well-being. It is much more difficult to determine the impacts of the latter. In truth, ecologists and conservationists have struggled to demonstrate the increased material benefits to humans of "intact" wild systems over largely anthropogenic [those derived from human efforts] ones. In terms of the most direct benefits, the reverse is indeed obviously the case; this is the logic that has driven us to convert some 1.5 billion ha [3.7 billion acres] of land area to highly productive, managed, and generally low-diversity systems under agriculture. Even with regard to indirect ecological services, such as carbon sequestration, regulation of water flow, and soil retention, it seems that there are few cases in which these cannot adequately be provided by managed, generally low-diversity, systems. Where increased benefits of natural systems have been shown, they are usually marginal and local.

Nowhere is this more starkly revealed than in the extinction of species. There is growing consensus that from around 40,000 to 50,000 years ago onward, humans have been directly or indirectly responsible for the extinction in many parts of the world of all or most of the larger terrestrial animal species. Although these species were only a small proportion of the total number of species present, they undoubtedly exerted a major ecological influence. This means that the "natural" systems we currently think of in these parts of the world (North and South America, Australasia, and virtually all oceanic islands) are nothing of the sort, and yet they still function at least according to our perceptions and over the time scales we are currently capable of measuring. In one well-documented case, New Zealand, a flightless avifauna of at least 38 species has been reduced in a few centuries to 9, most of which are endangered. Here, as David Steadman recently put it, "much of the biodiversity crisis is over. People won: native plants and animals lost". Yet, from a functional perspective, New Zealand shows few signs overall of suffering terminal crisis. There is currently little evidence to dissuade us from the view that what applies for New Zealand today could equally hold, more or less, for the world as a whole tomorrow.

This does not mean, of course, that we can continue to manipulate or abuse the biosphere indefinitely. At some point, some threshold may be crossed, with unforeseeable but probably catastrophic consequences for humans. However, it seems more likely that these consequences would be brought about by other factors, such as abrupt climate shifts, albeit ones in which ecosystem changes may have played a part.

Periodical Bibliography

The following articles have been selected to supplement the diverse views presented in this chapter.

Audubon	"Losing Ground: The Top 10 Common Birds in Decline," vol. 109, no. 4, July–August 2007.
Capper's	"Bald Eagle Taken Off Threatened Species List," August 2007.
Economist	"More of a Whimper: Asia's Last Lions," May 26, 2007.
Charlie Furniss	"Sea Change: The World's Commercial Fisheries Are in Terminal Decline," *Geographical*, vol. 79, no. 2, February 2007.
Michael Gallis, Gary Moll, and Heather Millar	"How the Human 'Network' Collided with the Environment," *American Forests*, Spring 2007.
Josie Glausiusz	"Across the Country Honeybees Are Vanishing: What Will Farmers Do If the Buzzing Stops?" *Discover*, vol. 28, no. 7, July 2007.
Jeremy Laurance	"Extinct: The Dolphin That Could Not Live Alongside Man," *Independent*, August 8, 2007.
Paul Raffaele	"Curse of the Devil's Dogs," *Smithsonian*, vol. 38, no. 1, April 2007.
Haider Rizvi	"Greedy Cities Consume Earth's Resources," *Mail & Guardian Online*, April 25, 2007.
Sports Afield	"Wolves Delisted: Recovery Deemed a Success," June–July 2007.
Robin S. Waples, Peter B. Adams, James Bohnsack, and Barbara L. Taylor	"A Biological Framework for Evaluating Whether a Species Is Threatened or Endangered in a Significant Portion of Its Range," *Conservation Biology*, vol. 21, no. 4, August 2007.

CHAPTER 2

Is Global Warming Endangering Plant and Animal Species?

Chapter Preface

In 2007 the Intergovernmental Panel on Climate Change (IPCC), established in 1988 by the World Meteorological Organization and the United Nations Environment Programme to evaluate and report the latest scientific findings on global warming, released its Fourth Assessment Report (AR4). The report predicts an average global temperature rise of between 1.8°C and 6.4°C during the twenty-first century, primarily due to greenhouse gas emissions produced by human activity. Most studies conclude the high estimate is far more likely than the low estimate; a temperature increase in the range of 6°C would result in an Earth warmer than it has been for at least 55 million years.

Many scientists contend that this much warming, unprecedented in human history, would have profound geological, geographical, and atmospheric effects, with potentially devastating consequences for the planet's animal and plant species. According to Ian Sample, the science correspondent for the British newspaper the *Guardian*, climate scientists have identified twelve global ecological weak links where "global warming could bring about the sudden, catastrophic collapse of vital ecosystems. The consequences will be felt far and wide."

John Schellnhuber, research director at the Tyndall Centre for Climate Change Research in Norwich, England, developed the following "tipping points, the Achilles' heels of the planet." The tipping points, and Schellnhuber's predictions about their effects on living organisms, are:

- Sahara Desert: Greening of the desert means the death of ocean plankton and organisms up the food chain, more severe storms, and crop devastation from locust infestations;

- Ozone Hole: Increased incidence of skin cancer and blindness;

- Greenland Ice Sheet: Flooding and displacement of inhabitants of the world's coastal zones;

- Tibetan plateau: Ice melt no longer capable of reflecting sunlight could wipe out species and exacerbate warming;

- Salinity valves: Shifting ocean currents would disrupt marine ecosystems adapted to zones where seas of different salinity meet;

- North Atlantic current: The oceans' "conveyor belt" would stop, driving frigid climate change in Scandinavia and Great Britain;

- El Niño: Changing weather patterns would disrupt agriculture;

- West Antarctic ice sheet: Melting would swamp the world's coastal regions;

- Methane clathrates: Toxic to many species, these chemical compounds, released into the atmosphere by the rupture of permafrost, could increase global warming by 25 percent;

- Monsoons: Would weaken, with serious disruption of Asian agriculture;

- Atlantic circumpolar current: Increased rainfall at the poles, harmful to marine species.

The viewpoints in this chapter debate the nature and extent of ecological damage caused by global warming and consider humankind's capacity to withstand and adapt to it.

"Approximately 20–30% of plant and animal species assessed so far are likely to be at increased risk of extinction if increases in global average temperature exceed 1.5–2.5°C."

Global Warming Will Accelerate Species Decline

Intergovernmental Panel on Climate Change

In 1988, the United Nations Environment Programme (UNEP) and the World Meteorological Organization (WMO) established the Intergovernmental Panel on Climate Change (IPCC) to assess the extent, impact, and mitigation of human-induced climate change. The IPCC analyzes and synthesizes the scientific, technical, and socioeconomic data of the world's researchers and publishes a comprehensive, peer-reviewed assessment. This viewpoint is a summary of the findings of the IPCC Working Group II Fourth Assessment, or AR4, released in April 2007. The AR4 is unequivocal: Global warming is occurring, is caused by human activities, and puts 20 to 30 percent of known species at risk of extinction. According to the assessments, extinction estimates soar in some places: up to 60 percent in mountainous European regions and entire ecosystems in the polar regions. The assess-

Intergovernmental Panel on Climate Change, *Climate Change 2007: Impacts, Adaptation and Vulnerability*. Geneva 2, Switzerland, 2007. Reproduced by permission.

ment documents unprecedented stresses to biodiversity in terrestrial, marine, and freshwater ecosystems. According to the AR4, even the strictest mitigation efforts cannot avoid near-term negative impacts, so adaptation is essential; the implication is clear that unmitigated climate change will exceed humankind's ability to adapt.

As you read, consider the following questions:

1. How is global warming currently affecting terrestrial biological systems, according to the AR4?

2. What observed changes in marine and freshwater biological systems does the IPCC attribute to rising water temperatures?

3. What non-climate stresses increase species vulnerability to even small changes in average temperature, in the IPCC's opinion?

This Summary sets out the key policy-relevant findings of the Fourth Assessment of Working Group II of the Intergovernmental Panel on Climate Change (IPCC).

The Assessment is of current scientific understanding of impacts of climate change on natural, managed and human systems, the capacity of these systems to adapt and their vulnerability. It builds upon past IPCC assessments and incorporates new knowledge gained since the Third Assessment [in 2001]. . . .

Recent studies have allowed a broader and more confident assessment of the relationship between observed warming and impacts than was made in the Third Assessment. That Assessment concluded that "there is high confidence that recent regional changes in temperature have had discernible impacts on many physical and biological systems".

From the current Assessment we conclude the following.

Global Warming Is Undeniable

Observational evidence from all continents and most oceans shows that many natural systems are being affected by regional climate changes, particularly temperature increases.

With regard to changes in snow, ice and frozen ground (including permafrost), there is high confidence that natural systems are affected. Examples are:

- enlargement and increased numbers of glacial lakes;

- increasing ground instability in permafrost regions, and rock avalanches in mountain regions;

- changes in some Arctic and Antarctic ecosystems, including those in sea-ice biomes, and also predators high in the food chain.

Based on growing evidence, there is high confidence that the following effects on hydrological systems are occurring:

- increased run-off and earlier spring peak discharge in many glacier- and snow-fed rivers;

- warming of lakes and rivers in many regions, with effects on thermal structure and water quality.

There is very high confidence, based on more evidence from a wider range of species, that recent warming is strongly affecting terrestrial biological systems, including such changes as:

- earlier timing of spring events, such as leaf-unfolding, bird migration and egg-laying;

- poleward and upward shifts in ranges in plant and animal species.

Based on satellite observations since the early 1980s, there is high confidence that there has been a trend in many regions towards earlier 'greening' [the amount of green vegetation in an area based on satellite images] of vegetation in the spring linked to longer thermal growing seasons due to recent warming.

There is high confidence, based on substantial new evidence, that observed changes in marine and freshwater biological systems are associated with rising water temperatures, as well as related changes in ice cover, salinity, oxygen levels and circulation. These include:

- shifts in ranges and changes in algal, plankton and fish abundance in high-latitude oceans;

- increases in algal and zooplankton abundance in high-latitude and high-altitude lakes;

- range changes and earlier migrations of fish in rivers.

The uptake of anthropogenic [human-caused] carbon since 1750 has led to the ocean becoming more acidic, with an average decrease in pH of 0.1 units. However, the effects of observed ocean acidification on the marine biosphere are as yet undocumented.

Human Activity Is Causing Global Warming

A global assessment of data since 1970 has shown it is likely that anthropogenic warming has had a discernible influence on many physical and biological systems.

Much more evidence has accumulated over the past five years to indicate that changes in many physical and biological systems are linked to anthropogenic warming. There are four sets of evidence which, taken together, support this conclusion:

1. The Working Group I Fourth Assessment concluded that most of the observed increase in the globally averaged temperature since the mid-20th century is

very likely due to the observed increase in anthropogenic greenhouse gas concentrations.

2. Of the more than 29,000 observational data series, from 75 studies, that show significant change in many physical and biological systems, more than 89% are consistent with the direction of change expected as a response to warming.

3. A global synthesis of studies in this Assessment strongly demonstrates that the spatial agreement between regions of significant warming across the globe and the locations of significant observed changes in many systems consistent with warming is very unlikely to be due solely to natural variability of temperatures or natural variability of the systems. . . .

Fresh Water Resources

By mid-century, annual average river runoff and water availability are projected to increase by 10–40% at high latitudes and in some wet tropical areas, and decrease by 10–30% over some dry regions at mid-latitudes and in the dry tropics, some of which are presently water-stressed areas. In some places and in particular seasons, changes differ from these annual figures.

Drought-affected areas will likely increase in extent. Heavy precipitation events, which are very likely to increase in frequency, will augment flood risk.

In the course of the century, water supplies stored in glaciers and snow cover are projected to decline, reducing water availability in regions supplied by meltwater from major mountain ranges, where more than one-sixth of the world population currently lives.

Adaptation procedures and risk management practices for the water sector are being developed in some countries and regions that have recognised projected hydrological changes with related uncertainties.

Twenty to 30 Percent of Living Species at Risk of Extinction

The resilience of many ecosystems is likely to be exceeded this century by an unprecedented combination of climate change, associated disturbances (e.g., flooding, drought, wildfire, insects, ocean acidification), and other global change drivers (e.g., land use change, pollution, over-exploitation of resources).

Over the course of this century, net carbon uptake by terrestrial ecosystems is likely to peak before mid-century and then weaken or even reverse, thus amplifying climate change.

Approximately 20–30% of plant and animal species assessed so far are likely to be at increased risk of extinction if increases in global average temperature exceed 1.5–2.5°C [2.7–4.5°F].

For increases in global average temperature exceeding 1.5–2.5°C and in concomitant atmospheric carbon dioxide concentrations, there are projected to be major changes in ecosystem structure and function, species' ecological interactions, and species' geographic ranges, with predominantly negative consequences for biodiversity, and ecosystem goods and services, e.g., water and food supply.

The progressive acidification of oceans due to increasing atmospheric carbon dioxide is expected to have negative impacts on marine shell-forming organisms (e.g., corals) and their dependent species.

Food, Fibre and Forest Products

Crop productivity is projected to increase slightly at mid- to high latitudes for local mean temperature increases of up to 1–3°C [1.8–5.4°F], depending on the crop, and then decrease beyond that in some regions.

Species Cannot Adapt Quickly Enough to Survive Global Warming

Documented rapid loss of habitable climate space makes it no surprise that the first extinctions of entire species attributed to global warming are mountain-restricted species. Many cloud-forest-dependent amphibians have declined or gone extinct on a mountain in Costa Rica. Among harlequin frogs in Central and South American tropics, an astounding 67% have disappeared over the past 20–30 years. . . .

Although local evolutionary responses to climate change have occurred with high frequency, there is no evidence for change in the absolute climate tolerances of a species. This view is supported by the disproportionate number of population extinctions documented along southern and low-elevation range edges in response to recent climate warming, resulting in contraction of species' ranges at these warm boundaries, as well as by extinctions of many species. . . .

Although evolutionary responses have been documented (mainly in insects), there is little evidence that observed genetic shifts are of the type or magnitude to prevent predicted species extinctions.

Camille Parmesan,
"Ecological and Evolutionary Responses to Recent Climate Change,"
Annual Review of Ecology, Evolution, and Systematics,
December 2006, pp. 652–57.

At lower latitudes, especially seasonally dry and tropical regions, crop productivity is projected to decrease for even small local temperature increases (1–2°C) [1.8–3.6°F], which would increase risk of hunger.

Globally, the potential for food production is projected to increase with increases in local average temperature over a range of 1–3°C, but above this it is projected to decrease.

Increases in the frequency of droughts and floods are projected to affect local crop production negatively, especially in subsistence sectors at low latitudes.

Adaptations such as altered cultivars and planting times allow low- and mid- to high-latitude cereal yields to be maintained at or above baseline yields for modest warming.

Globally, commercial timber productivity rises modestly with climate change in the short- to medium-term, with large regional variability around the global trend.

Regional changes in the distribution and production of particular fish species are expected due to continued warming, with adverse effects projected for aquaculture and fisheries.

Coastal Systems and Low-Lying Areas

Coasts are projected to be exposed to increasing risks, including coastal erosion, due to climate change and sea-level rise. The effect will be exacerbated by increasing human-induced pressures on coastal areas.

Corals are vulnerable to thermal stress and have low adaptive capacity. Increases in sea surface temperature of about 1–3°C are projected to result in more frequent coral bleaching events and widespread mortality, unless there is thermal adaptation or acclimatisation by corals.

Coastal wetlands, including salt marshes and mangroves, are projected to be negatively affected by sea-level rise, especially where they are constrained on their landward side, or starved of sediment.

Many millions more people are projected to be flooded every year due to sea-level rise by the 2080s. Those densely-populated and low-lying areas where adaptive capacity is relatively low, and which already face other challenges such as tropical storms or local coastal subsidence, are especially at risk. The numbers affected will be largest in the mega-deltas of Asia and Africa, while small islands are especially vulnerable. . . .

Australia and New Zealand

As a result of reduced precipitation and increased evaporation, water security problems are projected to intensify by 2030 in southern and eastern Australia and, in New Zealand, in Northland and some eastern regions.

Significant loss of biodiversity is projected to occur by 2020 in some ecologically-rich sites, including the Great Barrier Reef and Queensland Wet Tropics. Other sites at risk include Kakadu wetlands, southwest Australia, sub-Antarctic islands and the alpine areas of both countries. . . .

Europe

For the first time, wide-ranging impacts of changes in current climate have been documented: retreating glaciers, longer growing seasons, shift of species ranges, and health impacts due to a heat wave of unprecedented magnitude. The observed changes described above are consistent with those projected for future climate change.

Nearly all European regions are anticipated to be negatively affected by some future impacts of climate change, and these will pose challenges to many economic sectors. Climate change is expected to magnify regional differences in Europe's natural resources and assets. Negative impacts will include increased risk of inland flash floods, and more frequent coastal flooding and increased erosion (due to storminess and sea-level rise). The great majority of organisms and ecosystems will have difficulties adapting to climate change. Mountainous areas will face glacier retreat, reduced snow cover and winter tourism, and extensive species losses (in some areas up to 60% under high emission scenarios by 2080). . . .

Latin America

By mid-century, increases in temperature and associated decreases in soil water are projected to lead to gradual replacement of tropical forest by savanna in eastern Amazonia. Semiarid vegetation will tend to be replaced by arid-land vegetation. There is a risk of significant biodiversity loss through species extinction in many areas of tropical Latin America.

In drier areas, climate change is expected to lead to salinisation [build-up of salt in soil] and desertification of agricultural land. Productivity of some important crops is projected to decrease and livestock productivity to decline, with adverse consequences for food security. In temperate zones, soybean yields are projected to increase.

Sea-level rise is projected to cause increased risk of flooding in low-lying areas. Increases in sea surface temperature due to climate change are projected to have adverse effects on Mesoamerican coral reefs, and cause shifts in the location of south-east Pacific fish stocks. . . .

North America

Warming in western mountains is projected to cause decreased snowpack, more winter flooding, and reduced summer flows, exacerbating competition for over-allocated water resources.

Disturbances from pests, diseases, and fire are projected to have increasing impacts on forests, with an extended period of high fire risk and large increases in area burned.

Moderate climate change in the early decades of the century is projected to increase aggregate yields of rain-fed agriculture by 5–20%, but with important variability among regions. Major challenges are projected for crops that are near the warm end of their suitable range or depend on highly utilised water resources.

Cities that currently experience heat waves are expected to be further challenged by an increased number, intensity and duration of heat waves during the course of the century, with potential for adverse health impacts. Elderly populations are most at risk.

Coastal communities and habitats will be increasingly stressed by climate change impacts interacting with development and pollution. Population growth and the rising value of infrastructure in coastal areas increase vulnerability to climate variability and future climate change, with losses projected to increase if the intensity of tropical storms increases. Current adaptation is uneven and readiness for increased exposure is low.

Polar Regions

In the Polar Regions, the main projected biophysical effects are reductions in thickness and extent of glaciers and ice sheets, and changes in natural ecosystems with detrimental effects on many organisms, including migratory birds, mammals and higher predators. In the Arctic, additional impacts include reductions in the extent of sea ice and permafrost, increased coastal erosion, and an increase in the depth of permafrost seasonal thawing.

For Arctic human communities, impacts, particularly resulting from changing snow and ice conditions, are projected to be mixed. Detrimental impacts would include those on infrastructure and traditional indigenous ways of life.

Beneficial impacts would include reduced heating costs and more navigable northern sea routes.

In both polar regions, specific ecosystems and habitats are projected to be vulnerable, as climatic barriers to species' invasions are lowered. . . .

Very Large Impacts Are Likely after the 21st Century

Very large sea-level rises that would result from widespread deglaciation of Greenland and West Antarctic ice sheets imply major changes in coastlines and ecosystems, and inundation of low-lying areas, with greatest effects in river deltas. Relocating populations, economic activity, and infrastructure would be costly and challenging. There is medium confidence that at least partial deglaciation of the Greenland ice sheet, and possibly the West Antarctic ice sheet, would occur over a period of time ranging from centuries to millennia for a global average temperature increase of 1–4°C (relative to 1990–2000), causing a contribution to sea level rise of 4–6 m [13–19.6 ft] or more. The complete melting of the Greenland ice sheet and the West Antarctic ice sheet would lead to a contribution to sea-level rise of up to 7 m [23 ft] and about 5 m [16.4 ft] respectively. . . .

Vulnerability to Climate Change Can Be Exacerbated by Other Stresses

Non-climate stresses can increase vulnerability to climate change by reducing resilience and can also reduce adaptive capacity because of resource deployment to competing needs. For example, current stresses on some coral reefs include marine pollution and chemical runoff from agriculture as well as increases in water temperature and ocean acidification. Vulnerable regions face multiple stresses that affect their exposure and sensitivity as well as their capacity to adapt. These stresses arise from, for example, current climate hazards, poverty and unequal access to resources, food insecurity, trends in economic globalisation, conflict, and incidence of disease such as HIV/AIDS. Adaptation measures are seldom undertaken in response to climate change alone but can be integrated within, for example, water resource management, coastal defence, and risk reduction strategies. . . .

Even the most stringent mitigation efforts cannot avoid further impacts of climate change in the next few decades, which makes adaptation essential, particularly in addressing near-term impacts. Unmitigated climate change would, in the long term, be likely to exceed the capacity of natural, managed and human systems to adapt.

"[F]auna throughout the world can benefit from higher temperatures, but these findings absolutely never receive a scintilla of coverage in major news outlets."

Global Warming Is Good for Plants and Animals

World Climate Report

The World Climate Report *is a biweekly newsletter of global warming skepticism published online since 1995. It is edited by University of Virginia environmental sciences professor Patrick J. Michaels, associate professor of climatology Robert C. Balling Jr., and Arizona State University Laboratory of Climatology director Robert E. Davis, whose positions are that climate change is an overblown issue and that "the best expectation is modest change over the next 100 years." In this viewpoint, the* World Climate Report *blames media bias for failing to report thousands of scientific journal articles that conclude plant and animal species are benefiting from global warming.* World Climate Report *points to studies of lizards in France whose fitness by every measure has improved in recent decades, and of 54 species of butterflies in the United Kingdom whose distribution and diversity have increased in areas where temperatures have risen.*

World Climate Report, "Some Good News For Christmas: Reptile and Butterflies Flourishing," www.worldclimatereport.com, Reproduced by permission.

As you read, consider the following questions:

1. What three measures of fitness did Chamaillé-Jammes et al. apply to French lizards to conclude that temperature increases benefit the species, according to the *World Climate Report?*

2. What time periods did Menendez et al. compare in their butterfly study, as noted by *World Climate Report?*

3. Researchers refer to the time delay between present-day temperature increase and future species extinction as "extinction debt." It is suggested in this article that there is likewise a time delay between present-day temperature increase and future species *increase*; what is this concept called?

How many times have you seen articles in newspapers about global warming causing the extinction of some frog, toad, lizard, butterfly, or you-name-it-species? If today's newspaper doesn't contain such an article, Google "Global Warming and Extinction" and enjoy over two million sites. Repeatedly, if you see "Global Warming" and any species in the title of an article, heaven help members of that species, right?

What is odd is that literally thousands of professional journal articles show that virtually all plants benefit from elevated atmospheric carbon dioxide levels with or without any increase in temperature. With all the goodness in the world of flora, why do the fauna of the planetary ecosystem seem so vulnerable? The dirty secret is that the literature is full of articles showing the animal kingdom benefiting from changes that are under way.

The Literature Shows Global Warming's Positive Effects

For example, a 2006 issue of *Global Change Biology* contains an article about global warming and a "positive fitness re-

"A Tremendous Boon to Mankind"

One of the most serious problems facing the growing population of the world is an adequate amount of freshwater. Global warming is a tremendous boon to mankind (and to wildlife) in solving this problem: seventy-five percent of the freshwater of our planet is now trapped in glaciers and ice caps, and our technology is insufficient to melt those. Global warming, however, will do that in a slow, predictable way. Pure, clean and abundant water—one of the most precious and essential resources of the healthy and happy lives of all people—we will soon have in increasingly happy amounts. . . .

The environment will be better as well. The number of trees on earth will increase as the glacial areas of our planet recede. Trees are natural purifiers of our air, and we will all breathe cleaner and fresher air as global warming enriches our lives. The water will become purer as well, because the water in the melting ice caps is much purer than our rivers and lakes today.

Bruce Walker, "In Support of Global Warming,"
Enter Stage Right, February 12, 2007. www.enterstageright.com.

sponse" in mountain lizards in Europe. Did these lizards not get the memo about extinctions? Maybe the lizards haven't read their e-mail about global warming making things tough on lizards around the world? If nothing else, these lizards have obviously not been reading newspapers over the past decade!

A team of scientists from Spain and France decided to study mountain lizards in southern France in an area that has warmed over the past few decades. Chamaillé-Jammes et al. begin their article stating "Assessing species' responses to climate change is one of the greatest challenges for ecologists because global warming is expected to be a major threat for biodiversity in coming years." That sentence could be used to lead off literally hundreds of articles every year. Next, they note that "A recent study showed that up to 37% of species on Earth might be threatened by extinction because of the recent rise in temperature." In that context, they state "isolated (e.g. island, mountain) populations or species with limited dispersal abilities appear at especially high risk as available altitudinal or latitudinal gradient is limited. Global warming-driven extinction in these situations indeed has already been reported." One would never expect at this point that they will conduct the study and learn how the mountain lizards are benefiting from warming.

They collected data on common lizards from southern France and found "that individual body size dramatically increased in all the four populations studied over the past 18 years. This increase in body size in all age classes appeared related to a concomitant increase in temperature experienced during the first month of life (August)." Further, they write, "[Y]earling snout-vent-length increased by about 28%. As a result, adult female body size increased markedly, and, as fecundity is strongly dependent on female body size, clutch size and total reproductive output also increased." They find that "[i]n the same time, adult survival was also positively correlated to the temperature in spring." They conclude that "[a]ll fitness components investigated therefore responded positively to the increase in temperature, such that it might be concluded that the common lizard has been advantaged by the shift in temperature." We sincerely doubt that the Chamaillé-Jammes et al. team won any awards with such a positive message about warming!

Species "Richness" Is Increasing

OK, so there is some lizard in France that is benefiting from warming, but what about the butterflies that seem in desperate straits. Butterfly extinction just seems so unacceptable—

they are pretty, harmless, loved by children—a perfect and innocent member of the biosphere, and therefore, a poster child for global warmers. A 2006 paper in the *Proceedings of the Royal Society* by a team of scientists in the United Kingdom has some interesting conclusions regarding butterfly response to warming.

[Rosa] Menéndez et al. investigate changes in species richness using the well-monitored British butterfly fauna that include 54 species (not including continental migrants). They note that "Britain is a relatively species-poor region due to its cool-temperate climate, and the butterfly fauna show a species-richness gradient, with more species found in hotter areas in the south." In this investigation, the team tests "whether average species richness of resident British butterfly species has increased in recent decades, [and] whether these changes are as great as would be expected given the amount of warming that has taken place." They "compare patterns of diversity in two periods, 1970–82 and 1995–1999, when butterfly distributions were recorded comprehensively."

Menéndez et al. conclude that "average species richness of the British butterfly fauna at 20x20 km grid resolution has increased since 1970–82, during a period when climate warming would lead us to expect increases." They interestingly note that many others use the term "extinction debt" to denote the time delay between environmental change and the extinctions that will eventually take place as a result of those environmental changes. They conclude, "Just as important in the context of climate change (and species invasions) are 'colonization lags' to denote the time delay between environmental changes and colonization events."

These two recent articles are among many that show that fauna throughout the world can benefit from higher temperatures, but these findings absolutely never receive a scintilla of coverage in major news outlets. If the studies on British butterflies or French lizards had come up with negative consequences of warming, you would have seen the results in your local newspapers. But good news about the environment seems to be unworthy news, everywhere except *World Climate Report*.

"The effect on native biodiversity can be severe . . . 42% of the species on the Threatened or Endangered species lists are at risk primarily because of non-indigenous species."

Global Warming Triggers Invasive Species to Spread and Wipe Out Native Species

Rhett Butler

Rhett Butler is the creator and publisher of Mongabay.com, an independent San Francisco-based Web site, originally dedicated to tropical rain forest and fish conservation, that has expanded to cover global wildlands and wildlife and global environmental science. In this viewpoint, Butler reports what happens when climate change extends the range of plant and animal species into new territory, and the "disproportionate damage" this can cause to indigenous species. Butler concedes that species spread is not necessarily a problem, but warns that a small percentage of immigrant species disrupt ecosystems and displace or destroy native species at enormous economic and/or environmental cost, and this trend is accelerated by global warming.

Rhett Butler, "Invasive Species May Increase with Global Warming," news.mongabay .com, October 13, 2005. Reproduced by permission.

As you read, consider the following questions:

1. How does Butler define an invasive species?

2. What is the primary way invasive species disrupt ecosystems, and how does the zebra mussel illustrate this problem, according to Butler?

3. How have warming oceans enabled Indian Ocean species to enter the Atlantic Ocean, according to researcher Luiz Rocha as quoted by the author?

Research published in *Molecular Ecology* suggests that climate change could trigger the expansion of invasive species into wider ranges. The study looked at the genetic history of a goby species in the Eastern Atlantic which appears to have expanded its range dramatically when the world warmed about 150,000 years ago.

The finding has broader implications beyond aquatic reef fish. Invasive species cause billions of dollars in damage per year. In the United States alone, the economic cost of invasive species—in terms of the damage they do and the expense of controlling them—is estimated at $137 billion a year, according to a study by Cornell University in 1999. Should global warming fuel the arrival of more non-native species, the cost—both economic and ecological—will likely rise as well.

Why Are Invasive Species So Destructive?

While ninety percent of immigrant species do no obvious harm to their new home environment, a small number do disproportionate damage. By definition, "invasive species" are "an alien species whose introduction does or is likely to cause economic or environmental harm or harm to human health." Invasive species disrupt ecosystems primarily by preying on local species and competing with native species over limited resources. The effect on native biodiversity can be severe—the Cornell study says that 42% of the species on the Threatened or Endangered species lists are at risk primarily because of

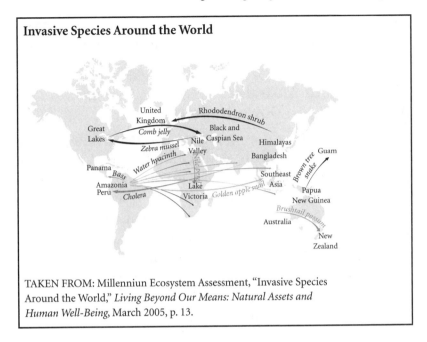

Invasive Species Around the World

TAKEN FROM: Millenniun Ecosystem Assessment, "Invasive Species Around the World," *Living Beyond Our Means: Natural Assets and Human Well-Being*, March 2005, p. 13.

non-indigenous species. Introduced tilapia and Nile Perch have devastated endemic fish populations throughout Africa, while the snakehead, a carnivorous fish capable of walking across land, has raised fears every time it appears in a pond in the Eastern United States. Further, there can be significant economic costs to the damage caused by such aliens. For example, removing the zebra mussel from the Great Lakes alone will cost $5 billion. The mollusk is a problem because it clogs water intakes for factories, interferes with navigation, accelerates decreases in fuel efficiency, damages engines, reduces the amount of food available for other filter-feeding organisms and fish, and competes with native mussels.

A warmer climate could mean more foreign tropical species could find their way to, and thrive in, the United States. Florida and Hawaii, the country's two most tropical states, have arguably suffered the most from invasive species. The python, a species of snake that has invaded the Everglades after pet owners have released it into the wild, has recently made headlines as it battles native alligators at the top of the food chain.

Cane Toads in Australia: Wreaking Havoc Down Under

Everyone in Australia is in agreement that the cane toads have got to go. The problem is getting rid of them. Cane toads, properly known as *bufo marinus*, are the most notorious of what are called invasive species in Australia and beyond. But unlike other species of the same classification, cane toads were intentionally introduced into Australia. The country simply got much more and much worse than it bargained for. Dramatic battles aside, the ecological and economic threat from invasive species is real and should serve as a reminder to what's in store for a warmer world.

Ocean Invaders in Deep Time

Much has been made of the economic impacts of recent biological invasions, but what are the implications of invasions in deep time? Luiz Rocha leads geneticists who time travel through ocean environments. The results of their travels, published online in *Molecular Ecology*, tell us that during warm, interglacial periods, reef-associated fish (goby genus *Gnatholepis*), leapt around the horn of Africa into the Atlantic, where their range expanded as the world warmed.

"We found that global warming events correspond clearly with major range expansions of gobies from the Indian Ocean into the Atlantic Ocean and subsequently into the Eastern Atlantic," summarizes Rocha. A chilly Antarctic current—the Benguela upwelling system—surges up along the western coast of Africa acting as a natural barrier, and has prevented most warm water organisms from the Indian Ocean from making it in to the Atlantic for the last 2 million years. But when the world warmed about 150,000 years ago, gobies slipped around the corner of the continent.

Researchers at the Smithsonian Tropical Research Institute, Scripps Institution of Oceanography, Hofstra University and the University of Hawaii, sequenced goby DNA (774 pb of the mtDNA of cytochrome b, to be exact) from the western, central and eastern Atlantic Ocean. They also sequenced DNA from gobies in the same genus from South Africa, from the Cocos Keeling Islands in the eastern Indian Ocean, and from the Cook Islands in the South Pacific. They calculated the approximate amount of time that isolated groups of fish have been separate based on the differences in the DNA between groups.

What evidence do they have that makes them think that Atlantic gobies are invaders? "The Atlantic goldspot goby certainly is a prime candidate—it's the only species of the genus in the Atlantic and there are eight species and subspecies in the Indo-Pacific. It's really similar to a sister taxon in the Indian Ocean," Rocha continues. "We nailed down the timeline of the invasion by sequencing—the last time there was tropical ocean connecting these two areas was 2 million years ago. We calculate that these fish invaded the Atlantic Ocean during a warm period about 150,000 years ago and arrived in the eastern Atlantic only 30,000 years ago."

Invasive Species Spread Will Worsen

What future effects of climate change might we expect in the marine realm? "Genetic analysis told us that fish from the Indian Ocean breached the Benguela barrier in the past, and this barrier seems to open intermittently. It would be reasonable to expect that other organisms limited by cold water barriers will continue to expand their ranges during warm periods."

> "[T]here is no scientific evidence of actual global extinction caused by a non-native species. Nor do exotic species threaten species 'richness' or 'biodiversity.'"

Non-Native Species Are Not Necessarily a Threat to Biodiversity

Dana Joel Gattuso

Invasive species are unfairly blamed for ecological damage and unfairly targeted for eradication by government agencies and environmental special-interest groups, Dana Joel Gattuso argues in this viewpoint. Gattuso maintains that it is pointless to label most species "invasive" because nearly all of the plants and animals in American food sources and gardens originated somewhere else and are benign. The few that are pests, he concludes, mostly cause commercial and agricultural damage, not species extinction. Moreover, he says, native species are just as likely to proliferate and evolve outside their natural habitat as exotic species, so costly legislation to control or keep out non-native species is a waste of taxpayer money. Dana Joel Gattuso is a senior fel-

Dana Joel Gatusso, "Invasive Species: Animal, Vegetable or Political?" *National Policy Analysis*, August 2006. Copyright © 2006 National Center for Public Policy Research. Reproduced by permission.

low at the National Center for Public Policy Research, a conservative think tank in Washington, D.C., that focuses on federal environmental and regulatory policy and national defense issues.

As you read, consider the following questions:

1. How many species does the U.S. Geological Survey estimate are non-native, and why is this a pointless exercise, according to Gattuso?

2. According to the author, what benefits of the Asian oyster, zebra mussel, purple loosestrife, and South American water hyacinth are overshadowed by bad press?

3. In Gattuso's view, why is the National Aquatic Invasive Species Act of 2005 bad legislation?

What do mute swans, kudzu, red clover, pigs, and starlings have in common? Not much, except that they are all non-indigenous species—that is, the species does not originate from within the United States.

And that is essentially all they have in common. Yet many government agencies, lawmakers and environmental special-interest groups would like to clump together the thousands of these species introduced within our borders and stamp out their existence. More than 50 bills are pending in the U.S. Congress to address so called "invasive species." Most bills would expand federal authority to further control land use and authorize billions of tax dollars to eradicate non-native flora and fauna.

Some "exotic species" are problematic, overtaking other species and imposing large economic costs in damages. But, contrary to public perception, these are more the exception than the rule. Most non-native species adapt to their surroundings, and many are even useful. . . .

Biased Definitions of "Invasive" Species

No one knows for sure how many non-native species exist in the United States. Documented estimates range from 6,500 by the U.S. Geological Survey to 50,000 from Cornell University. Still others assert these estimates are low because they don't include the numerous foreign species that are unknown.

One may wonder why the effort to quantify exotic species, given that just about all plants and animals, including the many we eat, grow in gardens and even keep as pets, hail from other parts of the world. The fact is that out of all the non-indigenous species found in the United States, only a tiny fraction are problematic. Out of these, "problematic" largely constitutes economic damage from clogged water pipes from aquatic foreign species, economic costs imposed on some commercial industries such as tourism and commercial or recreational fishing and costs to farmers for damage from non-native pests.

Yet many policy leaders and conservation activists lump all introduced species together and portray them as one of the biggest environmental crises of our lifetime. The National Park Service calls non-natives "one of the greatest threats to our natural and cultural heritage;" the Union of Concerned Scientists considers the intruders "one of the most serious and least-recognized tragedies of our time" and NASA calls them "the single most formidable threat of natural disaster of the 21st century."

There are currently 28 laws that pertain to the "control" of exotic species. The most recent—and far-reaching—is Executive Order 13112 on Invasive Species, signed by President [Bill] Clinton in 1999. The rule revoked an existing executive order signed by President [Jimmy] Carter that forbids the introduction of invasive species into U.S. ecosystems under federal authority.

The newer order granted new powers to federal authorities in an effort to wipe out not just foreign pests imposing economic damage but all "invasive species." The new, broader definition establishes that an "invasive species" is any "alien species whose introduction does or is likely to cause economic or environmental harm or harm to human health." Federal agencies were granted new, expansive authorities that can be applied to private as well as public lands to control and "minimize" species impacts and restore local species and their habitat to affected ecosystems.

The executive order also created the Invasive Species Council to monitor invasives' impact, develop a network for information sharing among government agencies, and come up with recommendations for eradicating the species or "preventing their spread." Under the order and other laws, more than 20 government agencies are responsible for some aspect of invasive species "management," with seven agencies—including the Department of Defense—spending over $1 billion a year.

Given that the executive order's revised definition of invasives covers just about every known species, it is no surprise that these demons are attributed with a wide range of crimes, including not only clogged pipes, power outages and agriculture disturbances but also spread of disease, collapse of buildings, threat to the world's ecosystems and even the "leading cause of extinction worldwide." Estimates on the amount of damages amounts to anywhere from $100 billion to $200 billion a year.

Hype and Hyperbole Over "Invading Aliens"

Some invasives, to be sure, are destructive, imposing high economic costs on numerous commercial industries. Farmers face myriad non-indigenous pests, for example, and the worst of them, like crop weeds, rats, gypsy moths and Mediterranean fruit flies, can imperil crops and jack up food prices. Aquatic non-indigenous species that can out-compete small-mouth bass, trout and other fish populations are hurting both the commercial and recreational fishing industries, particularly in

the Great Lakes region. Forests are prey to many foreign predators, including the Asian longhorn beetle and gypsy moth.
And a vast assortment of invaders in Hawaii impact tourism,
agriculture, and fishing industries.

The same can be said of native species that proliferate and
easily evolve outside their natural habitat. Most are harmless
and even beneficial while some can wreak costly havoc, such
as rabbits, white-tailed deer, barnacles and even native ticks
that can carry disease.

The well-kept secret about exotic species is that cases of
destruction are the exception; most non-indigenous species
are benign. As a report by the Congressional Research Service
states: "While the damage from some non-native species can
be great, few have proved to be economically harmful, and
many are beneficial."

In short, most of the costs imposed from a small percentage of non-native species affect select businesses and industries. They are not the national calamity portrayed by the
many interest groups that benefit from tax dollars and expanded government authority on lands where non-natives are
found.

Many Invasives Were Intentionally Brought Here

Many invasives were brought here intentionally, despite the
billions of tax dollars now spent to keep them out. Kudzu,
nicknamed "the vine that ate the South," was brought to the
region to control soil erosion. European starlings were brought
here in 1890 by a Shakespeare-enthusiast to introduce bird
species ever mentioned by the Bard to the United States. Asian
carp, prevalent in the Mississippi River Basin and the target of
numerous federal and state regulatory bills, were brought here
in the 1960s and 1970s to control algae throughout the South's
lakes and ponds.

Rarely mentioned are the numerous industries that rely on non-indigenous species, including nurseries, aquaculture, and exotic pets. Moreover, numerous states honor non-native species as their State Flower or State Birds. Vermont's red clover, Maryland's black-eyed Susan, California's poppy and South Dakota's ring-necked pheasant are all "invasive" species.

The wide range of benefits from many "invasives" is both well-documented and under-reported. Asian oysters, for example, are better at filtering out water pollutants than native oysters. They also grow faster and withstand disease better than natives. Biologists are currently considering releasing the mollusk in the Chesapeake Bay to help restore oyster stocks and clean up the bay's pollution. A recent study by the Johns Hopkins School of Public Health found the Asian oyster could significantly benefit the bay's deteriorating water quality.

In fact, invasives have become such a common part of our environment, culture and even diet that we don't think about them. For example, soybeans, kiwi fruit, wheat and all livestock except the turkey are exotic species. Collectively, non-native crops and livestock comprise 98 percent of our food system. These and other benefits from invasives are so vast that, according to the Congressional Research Service, they probably exceed the costs. Regrettably, benefits are rarely considered in reports and studies on the species' impact; nor are benefits much reported in news stories and articles on non-indigenous species.

Many Invasives Are Beneficial

The zebra mussel, for example, is one of the most feared "invasives," referenced in almost any article on exotic species and the purported raison d'etre for numerous bills pending in the U.S. Congress and state legislatures. The tiny mollusk inhabits fresh water lakes and rivers and is infamous for clogging industrial plant water pipes, particularly in the Great Lakes and Mississippi Basin, where they have exploded on the scene. Be-

Non-Native Species Increase Biodiversity

We have reaped enormous benefits from non-native species. Ninety-nine percent of crop plants in the United States are non-native, as are all our livestock except the turkey. "There is no basis in either economic or ecological theory for preferring native species over non-native species," said [University of Maryland philosopher Mark] Sagoff. He further challenged his fellow panelists [at a 2000 scientific symposium] to name any specifically ecological criterion by which scientists can objectively determine whether an ecosystem whose history they don't know has been invaded or not. Are invaded ecosystems less productive? No. Are they less species-rich? No. And so on. Tellingly, the panelists had to agree that there is no objective criterion for distinguishing between "disturbed" ecosystems and allegedly pristine ones. . . .

From a strictly ecological point of view, should we care whether a species arrives on a piece of driftwood or on a cargo boat? Why not just regard the introduction of non-native species as fascinating experiments? *Science* magazine estimated [in 1999] that 99 percent of all the biomass—that is, the total of all living matter—in some parts of the San Francisco Bay belongs to non-native species. Yet native species continue to live in the Bay. University of California at Davis evolutionary biologist Geerat Vermeij concluded in a 1991 *Science* article: "Invasion usually results in the enrichment of biotas [the total flora and fauna] of continents and oceans." In layman's terms, introducing species tends to raise the total number of species living in a given ecosystem, not decrease it.

Ronald Bailey, "Bio-Invaders," Reason,
August/September 2000. www.reason.com.

lieved by scientists to have been brought over from Europe in ships' ballast waters, some observers claim these hardy, prolific shellfish could wipe out native aquatic life, though there is no conclusive evidence to support this theory.

Rarely reported is the zebra mussel's positive effect on water quality. These "filter feeders" eat algae and fertilizer runoff from lakes and, as a result, waters they populate are frequently clear and free of pollution. As reported by the U.S. Geological Survey:

> There has been a striking difference in water clarity improving dramatically in Lake Erie, sometimes four to six times what it was before the arrival of zebra mussels. With this increase in water clarity, more light is able to penetrate deeper, allowing for an increase in aquatic plants. Some of these macrophyte beds have not been seen for many decades due to changing conditions of the lake mostly due to pollution. The macrophyte beds that have returned are providing cover and acting as nurseries for some species of fish.

The plant purple loosestrife, maligned for crowding out natural wetlands vegetation and wildlife, has been called everything from "the poster child" for invasive species to the "purple plague." Yet there is no scientific evidence that the plant causes actual displacement in the life cycle of native flora or fauna. Moreover, some biologists acknowledge actual benefits, including the plant's ability to absorb nitrogen and phosphorus from the water better than even cattails and to help prevent soil erosion.

Similarly, the South American water hyacinth blankets lakes and ponds in tropical climates, halting boat activity and, some claim, depleting aquatic life by blocking sunlight and crowding out native plant life. But the plant also has a newly discovered talent—it eats raw sewage. The alien species is used by a growing number of sewage treatment plants around the country to help purify water and performs the job at a fraction of the cost of conventional methods. NASA, which is researching the new-found technology, planted water hyacinth over 40 acres of sewage lagoons and reports: "The Plants flourished on the sewage and the once-noxious test area became a clean aquatic flower garden." They are also being researched for fertilizer, animal feed and biofuel.

Threat to Biodiversity?

Among the exaggerated claims regarding non-indigenous species is their alleged threat to the variety of species within ecosystems. According to Defenders of Wildlife, "The spread of non-native or 'exotic' species has emerged in recent years as one of the most serious threats to biodiversity, undermining the ecological integrity of many native habitats and pushing some rare species to the edge of extinction." The Nature Conservancy lists invasives second, just after species' habitat loss, as the biggest danger to biodiversity.

To be sure, there are cases where exotic species have eliminated local flora and fauna, out-competing them for food, oxygen or sunlight; the same can be said of some resilient native species too. But there is no scientific evidence of actual global extinction caused by a non-native species. Nor do exotic species threaten species "richness" or "biodiversity."

In fact, some scientists believe non-natives enhance diversity. According to Michael Rosenzweig, a biologist at the University of Arizona and the editor of *Evolutionary Ecology Research*, the presence of exotic species can actually lead over time to a greater number of species because the destruction of local species would allow for the introduction of new species. Similarly, evolutionary biologist Gereet Vermeij wrote in *Science*, "Invasion usually results in the enrichment of biotas [plant and animal life of a particular region] of continents and oceans. In some biotas . . . interchange has pushed diversity to levels higher than the pre-extinction number of species."

Where's the Science?

Xenophobia—an unfortunate tendency of some unthinking humans to dislike things foreign—has given non-native plants and animals a bad name. The media, some researchers, and environmental interest groups are largely to blame, raising the level of hysteria by playing on public fears with articles and books that evoke images of attacking aliens that, left unchecked, will multiply and conquer life as we know it.

Consider typical headings: "Giant rats invade Florida Keys: 9-pound rodents could threaten native species," "Sironga swamp threatened as 'magic tree' swallows up rivers," and "Killer Algae." Not surprisingly, emotion rather than science is driving government policy over how to handle these feared aliens. Missing from the debate are questions like: Is this a serious problem that extends beyond disruptions for some commercial industries? What are the benefits of non-indigenous species, and how do they stack up against the costs? What are the costs of widespread intervention, and is it justified? Who are the real players behind the "invasive species" hysteria, and how do they benefit from government regulations and intrusion?

Furthermore, existing laws and pending legislation apply the flawed, better-safe-than-sorry "precautionary principle," holding that we should first assume all invasives are damaging until we prove otherwise even though only a small percent of non-native species cause significant damage.

Legislation: Washington Goes to War

In spite of the fact that most non-native species are harmless, lawmakers are reacting to hype and exaggerations, launching numerous bills that, if passed, would cost taxpayers billions of dollars, assign government agencies a host of responsibilities aimed at eradicating "invasives" and preventing their spread, and expand government's authority over land use control. Consider:

S. 770, the National Aquatic Invasive Species Act of 2005: The bill, according to its sponsor, Senator Carl Levin (D-MI), is a "comprehensive approach towards addressing aquatic nuisance species." It attempts to prevent the introduction of aquatic invasives into the United States, screen all species entering intentionally, launch a national system for identifying introduced non-natives, establish a "rapid response" fund within the U.S. Treasury to aid states and non-government organizations (NGOs) that have detected a non-native "emergency" and earmark $30 million a year for "research, education and outreach."

The bill reads more like a plan to prepare the nation for an apocalyptic attack from aliens than to prevent damage from fingernail-sized mussels and waterweeds. Homeland Security would be given new authority to police vessels' ballast waters, side-tracking the agency's focus on terrorists to cover a very different class of invader.

"Aquatic" refers not just to oceans and lakes but to tributaries, wetlands, riverbanks and creeks—on private as well as public lands. The bill also applies the "precautionary principle," requiring the Fish and Wildlife Service to prove the species is not harmful if it determines to take no action. Moreover, the meaning of harmful is expanded to apply to change in the "structure and functions of ecosystems." . . .

Oversimplification of the Issue

The key problem with government's handling of the issue of non-natives is that it takes a simplistic view, bundling all the species together and exaggerating their effects on ecosystems and commercialism; if they come from outside our borders, we must assume they are harmful until we have evidence to prove otherwise. Resulting legislation such as those referenced above grant government sweeping authority, threaten property rights and authorize billions of taxpayer dollars when the actual problem is a small number of non-native species that impact the economic interests of some commercial industries.

Like snowflakes, no two species are alike. As stated by Mark Davis, an expert on invasives at Macalester College in St. Paul, Minnesota, "There are not generic conclusions we can make about invasive species. Each species really has to be approached uniquely." Furthermore, species' relationship within an eco-system is extremely complex and can vary enormously from one ecosystem to another. To address these unique circumstances, legislation should be case-specific, weigh species' benefits against costs, and should be based on peer-reviewed scientific evidence.

Periodical Bibliography

The following articles have been selected to supplement the diverse views presented in this chapter.

Chris Clarke   "No More Joshua Trees?" *Earth Island Journal*, Spring 2007.

Joe Dupree   "Coral Crisis," *National Wildlife*, June/July 2007.

Greg Easterbrook   "Global Warming: Who Loses—and Who Wins?" *Atlantic Monthly*, April 2007.

Geographical   "Wither Our Woodlands?" vol. 79, no. 5, May 2007.

Wayne Hsiung and Cass Sunstein   "Climate Change and Animals," *University of Pennsylvania Law Review*, June 2007.

Jason Scott Johnston   "Desperately Seeking Numbers: Global Warming, Species Loss, and the Use and Abuse of Quantification in Climate Change Policy Analysis," *University of Pennsylvania Law Review*, June 2007.

Frank Keppler and Thomas Rockmann   "Methane, Plants, and Climate Change," *Scientific American*, February 2007.

J. Madeleine Nash   "Chronicling the Ice," *Smithsonian*, July 2007.

Sid Perkins   "Stunting Growth: Ozone Will Trim Plants' Carbon-Storing Power," *Science News*, July 28, 2007.

Ian Sample   "Death in the Rainforest: Fragile Creatures Give the World a New Climate Warning," *Guardian*, April 17, 2007.

Erica Westly   "It's the End of the World As We Know It (and I, er, Feel Warm)," *Discover*, July 2007.

World Wildlife Fund   "Going, Going, Gone: Climate Change and Global Glacier Decline," 2007.

CHAPTER 3

Are International Efforts to Preserve Endangered Species Effective?

Chapter Preface

The Convention on International Trade in Endangered Species of Wild Fauna and Flora (CITES) is the primary international agreement regulating the transport and trade of endangered species around the world. For more than thirty-five years, CITES (today with 172 signatories) has maintained databases of rare and endangered plants and animals and set export quotas and guidelines for their sale and transport. A managing authority in each member country (in the United States, the U.S. Fish and Wildlife Service) works to keep one step ahead of determined smugglers, poachers, traders, and collectors, who find and sell live and dead animals as well as animal parts, in species' home countries and in more or less public city markets around the world.

CITES has recently been forced to enter a new arena—the Internet—where the illegal trade in endangered wildlife, timber, and other natural resources is flourishing. Internet transactions are largely unregulated, impersonal, instantaneous, private, and anonymous, and the Internet constitutes a single nonstop global marketplace without physical borders or border checkpoints, ideal conditions for criminal activity as well as convenient for buyers and sellers conducting legal business.

The International Fund for Animal Welfare (IFAW) conducted a three-month investigation of the illegal Internet wildlife trade to gauge the scope of the problem. For one week, in January 2005, IFAW monitored Internet traffic in five kinds of products and live animals: "live primates, elephant products, turtle and tortoiseshell products, other reptile products, and wild cat products." It was not possible to verify the authenticity or legal status of every sale item, but IFAW determined that the vast majority of goods came from legally protected species, and the sheer volume was stunning. "We found over 9,000 wild animal products and specimens and live wild animals for sale," the fund's report states. "The majority of these were offered for sale by private individuals":

> 5,527 individual elephant products and 11 traders [including] boots, wallets, purses, footwear, and bags; . . . ivory products such as jewellery, boxes, chess sets, ornaments, and expensive sculptures, including one with an asking price of US $18,000. . . .

> 146 live [primates] for sale on 15 websites, including baboons, capuchins, marmosets, vervets, tamarins, squirrel monkeys, bushbabies, lemurs, rhesus macaques and gibbons. . . . Four baby chimpanzees were offered on one USA-based site, while a seller in London was offering a seven-year-old gorilla.

IFAW argues that its findings represent the tip of the iceberg, as its narrow survey did not search for known high-volume trade in traditional Asian medicines containing wild animal parts or live birds.

One of the main channels for the illegal wildlife trade is the Internet auction site eBay. The IFAW's 2007 report on eBay sites in seven countries, "Bidding for Extinction: Wildlife Trade on the Web," takes the online shopping giant to task for lenient listing policies and inadequate oversight, but acknowledges that neither eBay nor CITES enforcement agencies have the resources to tackle the issue. The viewpoints in this chapter debate the effectiveness of international agencies' efforts to protect endangered species and offer strategies for improving their chances of success.

> *"The Endangered Species Act has been effective because it is based on good science."*

The Endangered Species Act Is Effective and Should Be Strengthened

Environment News Service

The Environment News Service (ENS) is the original daily international wire service of the environment. Established in 1990 by editor-in-chief Sunny Lewis and managing editor Jim Crabtree, it presents late-breaking environmental news. In this viewpoint, the Environment News Service discusses a 2006 letter to the U.S. Senate. This letter, signed by more than 5,000 scientists with biological expertise, supports the Endangered Species Act of 1973 (ESA) as the cornerstone of the nation's environmental protections. The signers urge legislators to maintain, strengthen, and fund the act, and to rely on the best available impartial scientific evidence, not on political special interests, in determining which species should be listed or delisted and how to best design recovery plans.

Environment News Service, "Scientists: Endangered Species Act Rewrite Must Be Science Based," www.ens-newswire.com, March 8, 2006. Reproduced by permission.

As you read, consider the following questions:

1. According to the author, what do the scientists who signed the letter fear about the Pombo bill?

2. How many listed species have gone extinct since the ESA was enacted in 1973, and how many candidate species have gone extinct waiting to be listed, and how do these events support the ENS argument that ESA is an effective law?

3. What new provisions did the environmental groups, businesses, academics, and foundations recommend for the ESA, according to the ENS?

Over 5,700 scientists with biological expertise have signed a letter to the U.S. Senate in an effort to ensure that the Endangered Species Act, which they call the "cornerstone of the United States' most basic environmental protections," continues to conserve biodiversity by using the best available science.

The letter, carrying signatures from scientists in every state and over 900 institutions, was hand-delivered to each of the 100 senators on March 8, 2006. In addition, several scientists personally delivered the letter and met with the senators and staff from their home states to discuss the importance of science and scientists to the Endangered Species Act.

Enacted in 1973, the Endangered Species Act (ESA) is up for reauthorization in Congress. A version passed in 2005 by the House of Representatives, and authored by California Congressman Richard Pombo, a Republican who chairs the House Natural Resources Committee, has been sent to the Senate. There it will come up first before the Environment and Public Works Committee.

Dangers of the Pombo Bill

The scientists who signed the letter fear that the Pombo bill undermines the role of science, shortens deadlines in a way that limits good science, includes new procedures that bypass key steps, and reduces the role of both scientists and science in managing endangered species.

"As Earth has changed and as science has progressed since the Endangered Species Act was authorized in 1973," they wrote, "the ESA has served our nation well, largely because of its flexibility and its solid foundation in science. It is crucial to maintain these fundamental principles. The challenges of effective implementation of the Act should not be interpreted to require substantive rewriting of this valuable, well-functioning piece of legislation."

In a telephone press conference, several of the signatory scientists said the Pombo bill limits the types species that can be protected and the circumstances in which they can be protected.

They warn that the Pombo bill prohibits the use of computer models in projecting the outcome of scientific management techniques.

Dr. Gordon Orians, Professor Emeritus of Biology with the University of Washington, said, "Pombo says thou shalt not use models, only empirical investigation, but everyone knows the only way to project future probability is that scientists must use models."

"We believe the major problem of the Endangered Species Act is not in its wording, but that it is seriously underfunded," Orians said. "Species become extinct while waiting for funding. The act should be properly funded so species that are on the list can be protected."

The ESA Must Be Strengthened

The letter, representing scientists from all 50 states and six National Medal of Science recipients, asks Congress to stop trying to weaken the Endangered Species Act and highlights the importance of independent scientific principles that are critical to species conservation.

The Endangered Species Act Works

Wildlife conservation has a long history in the United States, and the United States also is at the forefront of international efforts to protect wildlife. The federal Endangered Species Act (ESA) is the legal foundation for these activities. . . .

Many scientists credit the ESA with preventing the extinctions of the brown pelican, Aleutian Canada goose, peregrine falcon, bald eagle and the peninsular bighorn sheep. Populations of all but the latter two have recovered sufficiently to be removed from the list of species protected by the act. Other species, such as the masked bobwhite quail and the gray wolf, have been reestablished in the wild thanks to ESA protections.

Bridget Hunter, "Key U.S. Environmental Law Helps Save Species from Extinction," USINFO, April 20, 2007. http://usinfo.state.gov.

"By limiting the science that can be used to enforce the ESA, the House of Representatives has put endangered species at even greater risk," said Dr. Dennis Murphy, research professor at the University of Nevada, Reno, [in a] conference call. "Losing these species means losing the potential to solve some of the world's most intractable problems. Species diversity has provided humankind with food, fiber, medicines, clean water, and numerous other services that many of us take for granted."

"The Endangered Species Act has protected many species over the last 30 years. The bald eagle was on the brink of extinction in the 1970s and is now found in all the lower 48 states," said Dr. Jennifer Hughes Martiny, assistant professor in the Department of Ecology and Evolutionary Biology and Center for Environmental Studies at Brown University.

"The Endangered Species Act has been effective because it is based on good science," said Dr. Orians. "Since it was enacted, less than one percent of species listed under the ESA have gone extinct, while 10 percent of species waiting to be listed have been lost."

Supporting the Pombo Bill

But the Senate Republican leadership appears to approve of the Pombo bill. Senator James Inhofe, an Oklahoma Republican who chairs the Environment and Public Works Committee, commented in September 2005, "I share Mr. Pombo's belief that the ESA has not achieved all of its objectives and has, in many cases, led to dire consequences for landowners and species alike."

"I believe that it is essential that Congress pass legislation that would update and improve the ESA to focus on the recovery of species, while safeguarding private property rights. We should do this by working cooperatively with all stakeholders, especially private land owners on whose land more than 70 percent of species depend for their habitat," said Inhofe.

This position was underlined in a statement posted on the Environment and Public Works Committee website in the Republican section. It describes testimony given July 15, 2005 by Colorado Farm Bureau President Alan Foutz before the Senate Subcommittee on Fisheries, Wildlife, and Water about recovery of the mountain plover.

Due to a "strictly voluntary" study of the birds' behavior over three years by the the Colorado Farm Bureau, the Colorado Division of Wildlife, the Fish and Wildlife Service, the Rocky Mountain Bird Observatory and the Nature Conservancy, Foutz testified, researchers "found that rather than destroying habitat, agricultural activity actually provided important nesting habitat for the species, and many of the agricultural practices that would have been restricted under an ESA listing were actually beneficial for the plovers."

"The mountain plover success story would not have been a success if the plover had already been listed" under the Endangered Species Act, the press release states. Foutz testified, "This solution would not have been available to us if the mountain plover had already been listed. Under the ESA, once a species is listed, Section 9—taking prohibitions—and Section 7—consultation requirements—impose restrictions that stifle the kind of creative solutions that we employed to assist the mountain plover. Furthermore, had the mountain plover already been listed, we would not have been able to develop the scientific knowledge about the plover that could guide in its recovery."

The ESA Is Not Broken

But scientists who signed the letter delivered to the Senate believe that the Endangered Species Act is not broken.

"The Endangered Species Act is scientifically sound and its goals are important to human well-being. We should improve its performance, not reduce its protections," said marine ecologist Dr. Jane Lubchenco, who serves as Valley Professor of Marine Biology and Distinguished Professor of Zoology at Oregon State University, is a member of the National Academy of Sciences and a MacArthur Fellow, and past president, American Association for the Advancement of Science, Ecological Society of America, and International Council for Science.

"To weaken the scientific foundation of the Endangered Species Act is to doom more species to extinction," said ecologist Dr. Walter V. Reid, consulting professor, Institute for the Environment, Stanford University, who is also a former director of the Millennium Ecosystem Assessment, and past board member, Society for Conservation Biology.

Politics Should Not Trump Science

Dr. Stuart Pimm, who holds the Doris Duke Chair of Conservation Biology at Duke University, said [. . .] that the revision of the Endangered Species Act to exclude scientific processes is part of a wider attitude in the Bush administration that disregards science in favor of politics.

"We are very concerned that there has been an intrusion by the current administration to quite low levels of agencies to get the kind of science that fits their political priorities," he said.

"But it is 'broader than the Bush administration,' he said, and it is serious. We even have intelligent design people who want unverified data to be included in scientific studies."

In an attempt to bridge this gap, the Keystone Center held three consultative meetings from November 2005 through January 2006 at the joint request of Senators Inhofe and Lincoln Chafee, a Rhode Island Republican; Hillary Rodham Clinton, a New York Democrat; and Jim Jeffords, a Vermont Independent.

Joining the Keystone request were Senators Mike Crapo, an Idaho Republican, and Blanche Lincoln, an Arkansas Democrat, who introduced the Senate legislation to revise the Endangered Species Act.

They asked the Keystone Center to convene a working group representing all stakeholders. Co-chaired by Richard Burton of the MeadWestvaco Corporation and Rodger Schlickeisen of Defenders of Wildlife, the group addressed three questions:

1. As currently written and implemented, is the ESA adequately protecting and conserving the habitat listed species need to recover?

2. If not, how can the ESA be improved to better conserve habitat and help species recover?

3. What specific changes and recommendations can the regulated and NGO communities jointly recommend, advocate for, and help implement?

Members of the group, which included environmental groups, businesses, academics and foundations, concluded that the ESA is not protecting and conserving the habitat that listed species need to recover as effectively as it might.

Improving the Bill

Evaluating the discussions, Robert Olszewski, vice president of environmental affairs with the Plum Creek Timber Company, wrote, "The ESA is a critical piece of legislation to large land-owners as it impacts our operations daily. The Act is up for reauthorization and the Keystone Dialogue effectively brought together some of the country's best thinkers to discuss possible different approaches to the issue that could potentially improve both the plight of threatened and endangered species, as well as raising the level of certainty for private landowners in dealing with the implications of the Act."

"Conserving endangered species is becoming an increasingly difficult job, considering the increasing pressures on habitat from threats such as global climate change and human population growth. This Keystone dialogue will help Congress navigate this difficult terrain," wrote John Kostyack of the National Wildlife Federation.

The group recommended new provisions for integrating habitat protection and conservation into the Endangered Species Act to replace the current critical habitat framework; a greater focus on the function, content, scope, and mechanics of recovery plans; more effective incentives for non-federal parties, and new sources of funding for better coordinated and more workable ESA provisions pertaining to habitat.

"In its present form, the Endangered
Species Act must be regarded as a failure."

The Endangered Species Act
Is Ineffective and Proposed
Reforms Are No Better

Peyton Knight

*In this viewpoint, Peyton Knight condemns the Endangered Spe-
cies Act of 1973 (ESA) as a failure. Knight argues that the ESA
is responsible for the recovery of less than 1 percent of nearly
1,300 species given special protection, and most other listed species have declined further or are stuck in an endangered status
quo; political considerations, not objective reasons, determine
listing/delisting actions; ESA compliance costs billions of taxpayer dollars with little to show for it; and landowners are
forced to sign away their rights without fair compensation (or
their land use plans are stalled in bureaucratic limbo) when endangered species are identified on their property. The act's provisions, Knight contends, are so onerous that many landowners
"sterilize" their land to drive away the species in question rather*

Peyton Knight, "The 'Collaboration for the Recovery of Endangered Species Act': An
Analysis of the Senate Proposal to Reform the Endangered Species Act," *National
Policy Analysis*, June 2006. Copyright © 2006 National Center for Public Policy Re-
search. Reproduced by permission.

than lose control of their property, which only exacerbates species decline. Peyton Knight is the director of environmental and regulatory affairs for the National Center for Public Policy Research, a conservative think tank in Washington, D.C.

As you read, consider the following questions:

1. According to Knight, how many of the nearly 1,300 species have been delisted in the ESA's life span, and why have they been delisted?
2. What is the ESA's "perverse incentive problem," in Knight's critique?
3. What flaws does the author identify in CRESA, the Senate proposal to reform the Endangered Species Act?

In its present form, the Endangered Species Act must be regarded as a failure.

- After more than three decades, the ESA is responsible for the recovery of less than one percent of the species placed on its "endangered" or "threatened" lists;

- Changes to the "endangered" and "threatened" lists are at times years behind schedule;

- Political considerations at times replace objective or scientific reasons for listing/delisting actions;

- Most listed species are not recovering;

- The ESA's implementation is funded in an arbitrary manner;

- Aspects of ESA implementation appear to violate the Fifth Amendment to the U.S. Constitution.

Examine the Statistics of Species Recovery

In the more than 32 years the Endangered Species Act has been on the books, just 34 of the nearly 1,300 U.S. species given special protection have made their way off the "endangered" or "threatened" lists. Of this number, nine species are now extinct, 14 appear to have been improperly listed in the first place, and just nine (0.6 percent of all the species listed) have recovered sufficiently to be delisted. Two species (a plant with white to pale blue flowers called the Hoover's woolly star and a yellow perennial, Eggert's sunflower) appear to have made their way off the threatened list, in part through "recovery" and in part because they were not as threatened as originally believed.

A less than one percent recovery rate reflects failure, not success. Some environmental groups, however, insist that the ESA has been very effective. These organizations claim that since 99 percent of all species given special protection have either recovered or are still on the endangered and threatened lists, these species all "still exist" and, therefore, the ESA has worked. The "still exist" standard, however, tells us little about the true status of endangered and threatened species and certainly does not prove the efficacy of the ESA.

Recovery Is Not Necessarily a Result of ESA Listing

As the following examples demonstrate, the fact that a species has recovered does not necessarily say anything about the ESA:

- The Columbian white-tailed deer recovered primarily because of a refuge that was established prior to the ESA's enactment. Hunting restrictions also played a role, and could have been accomplished under laws that predate the ESA.

- The American peregrine falcon's recovery benefited enormously from captive breeding programs sponsored by The Peregrine Fund and other private organizations. Such programs would have existed without the ESA.

- The recovery of the Aleutian goose would have occurred without the ESA. The goose's decline was largely due to the introduction of a non-native predator, the Arctic fox, to the goose's island habitat. Once the foxes were removed, the goose again flourished.

- The American alligator's recovery had little to do with the ESA. There were already 734,000 alligators in 13 states by the time the ESA became law. Much of the alligator's recovery likely is due to a 1967 ban on alligator hunting.

A species' continued listing as "endangered" or "threatened" does not prove the ESA works. The goal is to recover endangered species, not to maintain the status quo.

ESA Listing Does Not Reflect Species' True Status

The "endangered" and "threatened" lists, moreover, are not well maintained. As the U.S. Fish and Wildlife Service noted [in 2005] in its rejection of a petition to delist the slackwater darter (*etheostoma boschungi*), petitions for delisting are frequently delayed "due to low priorities assigned to delisting petitions in accordance with our Listing Priority Guidance. . . . That guidance identified delisting activities as the lowest priority (Tier 4)."

Findings regarding delisting petitions are supposed to be made within 90 days. The slackwater darter petition was filed by the National Wilderness Institute on February 3, 1997, but this finding was not made until July 7, 2005, more than eight years later.

The act of delisting a species for any reason is so politically charged that it practically takes an effort equivalent to the passage of an act of Congress to get a species off the threatened or endangered lists. In July 1999, the Clinton Administration concluded that the bald eagle was fully recovered and should be delisted within one year. This was much to the chagrin of environmental activists, who didn't want the government to lose its regulatory authority over the bird's declared habitat.

In 2006 the bald eagle is still perched prominently on the endangered and threatened species list. Why the nearly six-year (and counting) delay? According to Jamie Rappaport Clark, executive vice president of Defenders of Wildlife and former Clinton Administration Fish and Wildlife Service director: "Partly it just fell through the cracks."

That the ESA has cracks large enough for America's national bird to fall through is proof enough the Act is flawed.

Yet it isn't only abundant species that fail to make it off the endangered or threatened list. By one estimate, 30 or more of currently listed species are extinct.

Even for species that aren't believed to be extinct, "existing" doesn't mean success, especially when species are hanging on by a thread. Just 36 percent of the species on the endangered and threatened lists are currently believed to be stable or improving—meaning that 64 percent are declining.

The "Perverse Incentive" Problem

Another ESA weakness is that the ESA's structure has worked against its success. The law pits species against landowners— often the very owners of the land on which rare species live. This adversarial relationship work's against the interests of both and is referred to as the "perverse incentive" problem within the Endangered Species Act.

The perverse incentive problem occurs this way: Those who harbor endangered species on their property, or merely own land suitable as habitat for such species, can find themselves subject to crippling land use restrictions. To avoid such restrictions and the losses in property values that accompany them, some landowners choose to preemptively sterilize their land to keep rare species away.

For example, when the federal government set out to protect the golden-cheeked warbler in the early 1990s, it did so by seeking to acquire land, through condemnation and other means, with mature cedar trees, the bird's favored habitat. Faced with the potential of losing their property, and their livelihoods, ranchers bulldozed cedar trees from their property.

ESA-related costs also are borne in a fundamentally inequitable way. Although Congress determined in 1973 that the preservation and recovery of endangered species was in the interest of the United States as a whole, it did not make arrangements for the nation as a whole to bear the costs of preservation and recovery. Instead, these costs substantially are borne by the private landowners on whose property rare species are found or may be found, regardless of the ability of any particular landowner to bear these costs. It is rather like funding a major national program by lottery: Lose in the lottery, and you pay, regardless of your wealth or income. Winners in the lottery don't have to contribute at all.

The "Threatened and Endangered Species Recovery Act," or TESRA

The ESA's poor performance and structure has prompted Congress to attempt to fix the law.

In October 2005, the House of Representatives approved TESRA. While not perfect, this bill has several strong points. TESRA would provide 100 percent, fair market value compensation to landowners who lose the use of their property due to ESA regulations. The ESA would then better comply with the Fifth Amendment to the U.S. Constitution, which stipulates that just compensation must be paid to those whose property is taken by government for a public use.

The House bill's fair compensation provision also would help species by eliminating perverse incentives within the current ESA.

"Collaboration for the Recovery of Endangered Species Act," or CRESA

In the Senate, Idaho Senator Mike Crapo (R) has introduced the "Collaboration for the Recovery of Endangered Species Act," known as CRESA. Unfortunately, CRESA does little to fix the ESA, and in some respects, makes it worse.

Among the key problems with CRESA:

- CRESA fails to provide fair compensation to land-owners who lose their property rights due to ESA regulations.

Landowners essentially would have two means by which they could attempt to receive compensation for their lost property rights under CRESA.

One option, which already exists, is for landowners to pursue compensation in court. This already has proven to be an expensive, drawn-out process with numerous bureaucratic roadblocks and zero guarantee of success. . . .

Alternatively, they could enter into a recovery agreement with the government for between ten and 30 years and only receive a tax credit worth 50 percent of any personal, out-of-pocket expenses related to the agreement. Under this agreement, the landowner would receive nothing in return for the lost use of his property. . . .

In a speech delivered at a U.S. Fish and Wildlife Service training seminar in 1994, Environmental Defense president Michael Bean spoke about how the ESA's perverse incentives have a detrimental effect on the red-cockaded woodpecker:

Because . . . red-cockaded woodpeckers tend to prefer . . . longleaf pine over other species, landowners thinking about what species to plant after harvest or on former forest land, any of them I think regard the choice of planting long-leaf as a foolish choice because of greater potential for having woodpecker problems in the future.

And because the Fish and Wildlife Service does not apportion foraging habitat requirements among adjacent landowners when an active colony of woodpeckers occurs near a property boundary, landowners have an incentive to be the first to liquidate their share of the available habitat before the Fish and Wildlife Service's minimum threshold of remaining habitat is reached.

Now it's important to recognize that all of these actions that landowners are either taking or threatening to take are not the result of malice toward the red-cockaded woodpecker, not the result of malice toward the environment. Rather, they're fairly rational decisions motivated by a desire to avoid potentially significant economic constraints. In short, they're really nothing more than a predictable response to the familiar perverse incentives that sometimes accompany regulatory programs, not just the endangered species program but others.

What is clear to me after close to 20 years of trying to make ESA work, is that—from the outside, in deference to you trying to do it from the inside—is that on private lands at least, we don't have very much to show for our efforts other than a lot of political headaches. And so some new approaches, I think, desperately need to be tried because they're not going to do much worse than the existing approaches. . . .

Habitat Designations Imperil Species, Not Protect Them

- CRESA would fail to eliminate costly, ineffective critical habitat designations and would imperil species by listing such designations on a public webpage. . . .

The ESA Is an Abject Failure

The abject failure of the ESA is a simple fact. Another fact is that 95 per cent of all species that ever lived on the earth have gone extinct. Darwin was right. Indeed, the history of biologic evolution is not one of equilibrium, but rather the result of every kind of natural calamity you can name. Does anyone really believe Nature is concerned for various species in the process of producing ice ages, volcanic eruptions, earthquakes or floods? In Iran, in late December [2003], an estimated 20,000 humans lost their lives to an earthquake [as did] untold numbers of wildlife from cockroaches to large mammals. . . .

Now here's something that will surprise you. Originally adopted in 1973, the ESA *expired* October 1, 1992! It continues only because Congress continues to fund it. There is not one single reason to fund a law that, during its lifetime, has "delisted" or removed from its "endangered" list only 25 species. Seven were removed due to extinction and twelve because the data suggesting they were endangered was proved to be "faulty", i.e., false. At last count, 1,853 species are listed as endangered or threatened. More than *4,000* species are designated "Species of Concern." With such a dismal record, one wonders why the ESA is permitted to continue.

Alan Caruba,
"The Endangered Species Act Deserves Extinction,"
Enter Stage Right, *January 12, 2004. www.enterstageright.com.*

CRESA would not only keep the ESA's current critical habitat program intact, but it would "publish maps and coordinates that describe, in detail, the specific areas that meet the definition" of critical habitat. CRESA also directs the Department of Interior to "maintain the maps, coordinates, and data on a publicly accessible Internet page."

Providing a public, online map of endangered species locations would be a convenient tool for endangered plant and animal thieves.

Like any rare commodity, endangered plant and animal species often are worth a premium. Unscrupulous traders and poachers covet them for the price they can bring on the black market.

In the Shawnee National Forest in Illinois in 1991, an entire population of threatened Mead's milkweed was stolen. Orchids, cycads, cacti and carnivorous plants are also prime targets for plant thieves and international smugglers.

Addressing the problem of plant and animal species being poached from our national parks, John Garrison, chief ranger at Blue Ridge National Parkway in North Carolina, said, "It's just of a magnitude most people can't comprehend, it's that widespread." . . .

"Paying Billions of Dollars for a Law That Doesn't Work"

The ESA's failure to protect private property has proven detrimental to both species and landowners. This failure comes at a steep price.

In 2004, the Fish and Wildlife Service and the National Marine Fisheries Services by themselves spent over $238 million on the ESA. Many other government agencies—from the Bonneville Power Administration to the Coast Guard to the Air Force—together spend hundreds of millions of dollars more on ESA compliance every year.

These government expenditures, of course, don't include the devastating costs to individual property owners who have lost their investments and their livelihoods in the name of species protection.

In fact, Americans are paying billions of dollars annually for a law that doesn't work.

The Property and Environment Research Center noted in a 2004 report:

> From 1989 to 2000, the FWS estimates that a little over $3.5 billion of taxpayer dollars was spent on ESA-related activities. We recognize today that the actual cost of protecting species, including private costs ... may easily reach or exceed that figure per year.

The ESA will not be fixed until private property rights are given full protection and the perverse incentives of the law are eliminated.

There are several ways to achieve this.

One way is to provide an economically viable means whereby landowners who lose property rights under the ESA can receive full and fair compensation for their losses in a timely manner. ...

Species Preservation Needs Stronger Private Property Rights

History has shown that secure private property rights and good environmental stewardship go hand in hand.

Environmental scholar Robert J. Smith points out:

> Why are some species disappearing and others thriving? First, we can examine what is disappearing and what is not. Why was the American buffalo nearly exterminated but not the Hereford, the Angus or the Jersey cow? Why do cattle and sheep ranchers over-graze the public lands but maintain lush pastures on their own property? Why are rare birds and mammals taken from the wild in a manner that often harms them and depletes the population, but carefully raised and nurtured in aviaries, game ranches, and hunting preserves? In all of these cases, it is clear that the problem of overexploitation or overharvesting is a result of the resources being under public rather than private ownership. The difference in their management is a direct result of two totally differ-

ent forms of property rights and ownership: public, communal, or open-access common property vs. private property. Wherever we have public ownership we find overuse, waste, and extinction; but private ownership results in sustained-yield use and preservation.

In its present form, the Endangered Species Act fails species and landowners alike. It will continue to do so until private property rights are given full protection and anti-species perverse incentives within the law are eliminated.

> *"Furbearers, large mammals . . . croco-dilians, and ornamental birds tradi-tionally impacted by wildlife trade ben-efited from CITES actions."*

CITES Is Slowing the Trade in Endangered Species

Peter Thomas

CITES, the Convention on International Trade in Endangered Species, is an international treaty signed in 1975 by 80 world governments to ensure that trade in wildlife species does not threaten the animals' survival. Today CITES has 172 member countries and accords protection to 5,000 animal species and 28,000 plant species, which are listed on one of three appendixes according to their threat of extinction. In this viewpoint, Peter Thomas of the U.S. Fish and Wildlife Service (FWS) argues that CITES has played an important role in conserving not only "poster child" species such as tigers and rhinos but also high-volume flora and fauna such as bluefin tuna and bigleaf ma-hogany. Thomas maintains that the agreement has genuine au-thority: Just the threat of CITES action, for example, led the U.S. government to improve existing tuna fisheries management.

Peter Thomas is management authority chief in the FWS Division of International Conservation in Arlington, Virginia.

As you read, consider the following questions:

1. What objections did member parties raise to CITES protection of mushooms and other fungi, and what is the status of this debate, according to Thomas?

2. In which appendix is the bigleaf mahogany now listed, according to the author?

3. In Thomas's view, how will the creation of the Bushmeat Working Group enhance CITES efforts in central Africa?

At the opening session of the twelfth meeting of the CITES Conference of the Parties (COP) in Santiago, Chile, in 2002, I listened in fascination as delegates from 160 member countries debated whether CITES should cover mushrooms. While no proposal to list fungi was on the table, the question arose over a possible proposal to list the American matsutake mushroom.

The treaty's title makes clear that it covers "trade in endangered species of wild fauna and flora." But did "flora" include mushrooms at the time the treaty was negotiated in the early 1970s? In 1961, taxonomists began to split the fungi into a separate kingdom from plants, a change that took some time, but the COP 12 debate centered on whether the original negotiators of the treaty thought it covered all plants in trade in the broadest sense. Japan and China did not think fungi fell within the jurisdiction of CITES and expressed doubt that any species of fungus was endangered by trade, an assertion questioned by Kenya, Mexico, and Peru. In the end, the Parties adopted a recommendation that CITES should be considered to apply to fungi, with a reservation by the delegation of Japan.

CITES Moves to Protect Commercial Fisheries

Whether this decision will lead to the listing of a fungus under the CITES appendices is still to be determined, but it reflects a broader trait of the CITES Parties. They are forward thinking and not afraid to move into new territory as they seek to protect species from overexploitation due to international trade.

During the first decade of CITES, Parties focused their conservation attention on the large number of species initially listed. Furbearers, large mammals (such as elephants, rhinos, and tigers), crocodilians, and ornamental birds traditionally impacted by wildlife trade benefited from CITES actions. However, in the late 1980s, as concern grew for the sustainability of fisheries and timber extraction and the impacts of such harvest on major ecosystems, proposals to list new, high-volume commercial species began to appear on the CITES agenda.

Such proposals generated great controversy, provoking questions of whether CITES was intended to deal with such species. When I began working on CITES in 1991, a proposal to list Atlantic bluefin tuna was being prepared by the United States. Within the U.S. government, experts differed on whether a CITES listing should supplant the fisheries management for tuna already in place.

At COP 8 in Kyoto, Japan (1992), the proposal was hotly debated. While the proposal was rejected, the continued threat of CITES action led to a change for the better in tuna management. Generally, when other management bodies are in place for marine species, the threat of CITES listing has motivated those bodies to enact or better implement sustainable management goals. Where appropriate management bodies don't exist, CITES has stepped in, as exemplified by the listing of the whale shark and basking shark at COP 12 and the great white shark and humphead wrasse at COP 13.

CITES and eBay Cooperate to Control the Ivory Trade

CITES banned the international commercial [elephant] ivory trade worldwide in 1989. But four southern African countries want to sell at least 60 tons of legally acquired ivory from healthy and well managed herds, saying they need the proceeds for conservation.

Other African range states and most environmentalists say that even a legal ivory trade will encourage elephant poachers.

Under the compromise by African range states [at the 14th CITES meeting in June 2007], each of four southern African countries will be permitted to make a single sale of ivory in addition to the total sale of 60 tons that was agreed in principle in 2002 and approved by the CITES Standing Committee on June 2, [2007].

After these shipments have been completed, no new proposals for further sales from these four countries will be considered by CITES during a "resting period" of nine years. Online auction site eBay said [on June 5] it will ban all international trading of elephant ivory in an announcement timed to coordinate with the CITES conference. The auctioneer said it would start the ban by the end of June [2007].

The International Fund for Animal Welfare, IFAW, said eBay's action is the first online international trading ban of elephant ivory.

Environment News Service, "CITES Decisions Map the Future of Wildlife Trade," June 15, 2007. www.ens-newswire.com.

Protections Extended to Timber Species

COP 8 also saw a proposal to list the bigleaf mahogany (Swietenia macrophylla) on CITES Appendix II. This was the first major commercial timber species to be considered for such a listing. The Parties could not agree to the listing, despite evidence of unsustainable and uncontrolled harvest.

At COP 10 in Harare, Zimbabwe (1997), a colleague and I had responsibility for marketing a new U.S./Bolivian proposal to list the species on Appendix II. We met unbending resistance from Brazil and could not achieve the two-thirds majority vote required. Finally, under threat of a call for a re-vote, we persuaded Brazil to join with other range countries to each list bigleaf mahogany on Appendix III, a measure that brought the trade under CITES review.

Eleven years after action on the tree was first proposed, with conservation concern still high and despite new measures in some countries (a moratorium on harvest and trade in place in Brazil), CITES member nations agreed at COP 12 to place bigleaf mahogany on Appendix II. The U.S. supported the proposal on the strength of scientific concern over the status of the species and the conviction that placing the trade under the unique requirements of CITES would support the efforts of range countries to base continued trade on legal and sustainable harvest.

I expect that CITES will continue to explore new arenas and consider new species for protection as threats from trade continue, as habitat degradation or destruction jeopardizes species already in trade, and as new species come under greater trade pressure. Versatility was a CITES trademark at its inception in 1973 and continues to characterize the treaty today.

Increasing International Cooperation

In 2001, the CITES Parties adopted a five-year Strategic Vision "to ensure that no species of wild fauna or flora becomes or remains subject to unsustainable exploitation because of international trade." One of the goals is to increase cooperation with other international organizations.

Many international organizations have sustainable development among their objectives, though emphases may vary. I have represented the U.S. during contentious negotiations on CITES and the U.N. Food and Agriculture Organization (FAO) regarding marine species. Along with sustainable development, FAO has strong food security, and commercial development goals, which some of its member countries (the major fisheries nations) see as at odds with CITES' sustainability efforts.

In contrast, strong collaboration among a variety of organizations has enhanced efforts to address the bushmeat crisis in central Africa. Bushmeat refers to any terrestrial wild animal, including elephants, gorillas, antelopes, and pangolins, used for food. At COP 11, the CITES Parties established the Bushmeat Working Group and invited other organizations, such as the Convention on Biological Diversity, to participate. Each organization in the working group has brought forward unique expertise to support regional efforts to tackle unsustainable harvest and trade in bushmeat.

No mushrooms may yet be listed on CITES, but the discussions that opened COP 12 highlight the willingness of Parties to conserve all living things at risk from the demands of international trade. CITES reminds us that all nations must contribute to the appropriate regulation of wildlife trade so that the diversity of the Earth will be sustained for future generations.

"[I]t is fair to say that CITES has not yielded a stable or improving situation for many of the most important wildlife of the world."

CITES Is Not Slowing the Trade in Endangered Species

Robert H. Nelson et al.

Robert H. Nelson is a professor in the environmental policy program at the School of Public Policy, University of Maryland. In this viewpoint, Nelson and graduate students in the school's policy analysis workshop argue that the the international Convention on Trade in Endangered Species (CITES), in force since 1975, is ineffective and fundamentally flawed, and recommend reforms to improve the chances of saving critically endangered species. The central problem, in the authors' view, is that developed countries make the rules and reap the benefits of wildlife resources but expect poor developing countries (where most endangered species live) to bear the costs, and then blame poor governments for putting human economic and social needs ahead of species conservation.

Robert H. Nelson et al., *The Convention on International Trade in Endangered Species: 30 Years Later*. College Park, MD: University of Maryland School of Public Affairs, 2003. Reproduced by permission of the author.

As you read, consider the following questions:

1. How do the authors use African elephants as an example of the problem that there is little motive to conserve a species unless it has economic as well as intrinsic value?

2. How do the authors recommend CITES should support genetic rights to wildlife, and how might this improve species survival?

3. Why do Nelson et al. oppose CITES's stricter domestic measures (SDM) provisions?

The Convention on International Trade in Endangered Species (CITES) was approved in 1973 and, after 30 years, it is appropriate to take a close look at the results achieved. It is notable that there have been few successes in the protection of internationally endangered wildlife. Most populations of critical wildlife species have declined, in many cases severely, but the declines might have been even greater in the absence of CITES. Nevertheless, it is fair to say that CITES has not yielded a stable or improving situation for many of the most important wildlife of the world. This is partly because CITES affects only one of the threats impacting wildlife—the trade in endangered species. It is also because CITES has a number of features that may be counterproductive to the goals of long-run species protection and preservation. . . .

CITES Imposes Unfair Costs on Developing Nations

The benefits of CITES are largely realized by the developed nations of the world, while the costs are largely borne by the developing nations of the world. In other words, the rich benefit the most and the poor pay the most. This is a fundamental problem facing CITES. In the absence of a more equitable distribution of benefits and costs, there is little prospect that CITES will achieve the objectives for which it was created. It is not only a matter of social equity, but also effectiveness. The poorer nations of the world will not take the steps necessary to protect their wildlife until they see a greater benefit for themselves. With large numbers of people living on the edge of survival, they have higher priorities than maintaining the "existence" or "intrinsic" value of world wildlife—a value that is highest in countries such as the United States and the member states of the European Union.

It is the developed countries that at present have the money and resources to conduct scientific studies, send large delegations to Conferences of the Parties (COPs), monitor trade, and undertake other activities related to the purposes of CITES. Yet, it is the less developed countries of the world that contain many of the most valuable wildlife populations from a worldwide standpoint. During the colonial era, these poorer countries had their policies for wildlife management imposed by their colonial overlords. Since the end of the colonial era, matters have not changed as much as one might have assumed. Today, many developing nations still find that the United States, the European Union and other richer nations are dictating their wildlife policies.

Until the governments and the peoples of the developing nations of the world develop a greater internal commitment to the preservation of world biodiversity, based on their own values and self-interest, the efforts of CITES and other international instruments will be swimming against the tide. A sustainable CITES—and sustainable wildlife populations—must reflect the political and economic objectives of the developing world as well as the desires of the richer countries. The developed countries, for their part, must make a greater commitment to meeting the wildlife needs of the poorer nations of the world.

A Vision of Sustainable World Wildlife

The conservation of endangered species cannot effectively take place without a mechanism to regulate international trade.

However, trade regulations should be considered as only a small part in an overall international effort for conservation. Even though CITES plays a small part in the international conservation of species, it is nonetheless critical that it be properly and fairly implemented. CITES certainly has some technical problems—for example, . . . implementing enforcement in poor countries. Besides dealing with the practical problems of CITES, it is necessary to rethink the basic philosophy of CITES—and to address the underlying conflict between the North and South. For the South, the very economic survival of human populations is often at issue; wildlife conservation necessarily takes second place to this concern. Yet, through CITES and their own stricter domestic measures, the developed nations often impose a priority of wildlife conservation over human well-being. This prioritisation is not intentional, but rather an unintended consequence of the clash between two different philosophies on conservation. In the long-run, this cannot be a sustainable strategy either for wildlife or the future existence of CITES. . . .

CITES will only be effective when it genuinely works in concert with national states rather than against them. There needs to be a higher degree of mutual respect for sovereign rights of nations and a tolerance of a wider variety of conservation approaches. In addition, the Parties need to determine ways for developing nations to have the economic means necessary to protect their wildlife while providing for the development of their own people. . . .

CITES Should Adopt a Philosophy of Sustainable Use for Wildlife

CITES should adopt a philosophy of sustainable wildlife use. Despite the good intentions of those who want to protect animals and plants for their intrinsic value, unless a species has economic value there is little motive for people to conserve it. Elephants may appear valuable to some, but certainly not to the subsistence farmers of Africa whose crops are trampled.

However, if the communities that live next to elephant populations can benefit economically from the elephants, they will value them. This also gives people incentives to work together to stop poachers.

If CITES is to be successful at protecting threatened and endangered species, it will need to consider resolutions such as the one proposed by Norway at COP12. At this meeting, the delegation of Norway introduced a document which stressed the importance of placing CITES in the context of sustainable development. The document also highlighted the importance of the synergy between CITES, the World Summit on Sustainable Development, the Convention on Biological Diversity and other multilateral environmental agreements through the development of guidelines that define sustainable use. The proposal included a "sunset clause" for automatic review of CITES Appendices for species not threatened by trade. Norway also introduced amendments to the proposal that included language on cooperation between CITES and the United Nations Food and Agriculture Organization (FAO), the application of the listing criteria in a manner that supports sustainable use, and considerations on sustainable trade and sustainable development. However, these measures encountered resistance and were not adopted.

To truly be a key player in the recovery of wildlife species, CITES needs to evolve towards a management regime. This report recommends the creation of a World Recovery Plan, under which individual nations would be responsible for creating and implementing their own National Species Recovery Plans. The CITES Secretariat would have authority to review these individual plans, and would be responsible for evaluating the success of the plans. In this way, CITES can contribute to a world management system that encourages individual countries in their wildlife restoration efforts. The individual countries, in turn, can create management plans that are compatible with their views on sustainable development and the needs of their people.

Developed Countries Should Pay Directly for Wildlife Protection Measures in Developing Countries

Developing countries should not have to incur the majority of the costs associated with species protection. These countries are often unable to incur such costs; therefore, expecting them to do so is unrealistic and detrimental to the overall effectiveness of the treaty. CITES needs to establish a stronger mechanism through which developed countries bear significantly more of the financial burden associated with the decisions of the Convention. This would make developed countries less willing to impose unworkable trade restrictions on species found in developing countries. Furthermore, if all of the Parties collectively paid the costs associated with species protection, CITES would become a more cooperative and more focused institution. If everyone shares the costs associated with CITES, the Parties would be more likely to work together, and to impose trade restrictions that are truly meant to protect species from overexploitation through international trade. In sum, the CITES process would be less likely to be excessively influenced by narrow Western politics and values if the developed countries were forced to pay more of the costs associated with wildlife protection in developing countries.

CITES Should Recognize and Support Genetic Rights to Endangered World Wildlife

While there is great interest worldwide in the preservation of biodiversity, this concern often fails to translate into substantial economic benefits for the nations that are host to many of the world's most important wildlife populations. This suggests that it may be desirable to create property rights—or the practical equivalent—to the biodiversity of the world. If nations, or individuals, are able to profit directly from enhanced wildlife populations, there will be a much greater incentive to preserve the world's endangered species. Accordingly, the United Nations Convention on Biological Diversity (CBD) has proposed that financial benefits derived from the research and development of a nation's natural genetic resources (such as development of pharmaceutical products from native plants) be shared equitably with the country possessing the resource. In a similar fashion, CITES should devise a strategy for animals that rewards nations that possess important genetic resources of endangered wildlife species. For example, the financial benefits from captive breeding operations might be transferred in part (perhaps through a royalty) to the species' home country. By promoting genetic property rights for commercially-bred animals, it would be possible for biodiversity-rich nations to benefit not only from their plant genes, but from their animal gene pool as well.

CITES Should Play a More Proactive Role

CITES should include a "World Species Recovery Plan" as part of each new animal species listing under Appendix I, and over time the Recovery Plans should be developed for all previous Appendix I animal species listings. The Plans would go well beyond the non-detriment standard of CITES. At present, the standard has no inherent criteria that look to the future of the population, nor does it have plans for an eventual down-listing of the species. The Recovery Plans should be designed for individual species, providing a recovery objective as well as a list of measurable criteria that indicate success. Success would be measured based on the determination that populations have achieved a self-sustaining level. A recovery plan may include different options, including reintroduction, habitat acquisition, captive breeding, habitat restoration and protection, population assessments, research and technical assistance for landowners, and public education. The development of such a Plan by CITES for species of world importance would follow after the model of the Endangered Species Act (ESA) in the U.S., where recovery plans must be prepared by the Fish and Wildlife Service for domestic-listed species.

CITES Should Integrate Its Work with Other International Wildlife Conservation Efforts

The workings of CITES should be integrated closely with other international wildlife efforts, such as those taken under the Convention on Biological Diversity (CBD) and the UN Food and Agriculture Organization (FAO). This integration would require a harmonization of the procedures that these regimes have in common, such as reporting and permit requirements. It would also require that CITES take advantage of those mechanisms and policies available in other international regimes that would further the goal of sustainable management of the world's biodiversity. For example, CITES should utilize the experience gained by the FAO in establishing sustainable use policies; the experience gained from the establishment of financial mechanisms for the CBD; the information obtained by the genetic, species, and ecosystem inventories required by the CBD; and the experience and information obtained by the CBD's National Strategy and Action Plans. In addition, the CITES Secretariat should work more closely with these international efforts. One example of the type of close collaboration needed is that between the CBD and CITES to address the threats to bushmeat. This type of collaboration and integration recognizes that international trade in endangered species is just one component of the problem of worldwide biodiversity loss. A fuller integration of CITES and these international efforts will provide a more effective solution to the problem than the patchwork approach currently in place. . . .

The United States Leads the World in Undermining CITES

Though CITES was originally intended to regulate wildlife trade, today both legal and illegal trading are at all-time highs. Improved transportation systems, booming economies in many parts of the world, increasing personal wealth, and an ever-expanding number of businesses selling or relying on wildlife or wildlife products are driving this trade to the detriment of wild species and their habitats around the world. In concert with a worldwide apathy regarding the destruction of our environment, as well as substantial profits to be made by governments and businesses engaged in wildlife trade, these are significant contributing factors to our worldwide biodiversity crisis. . . .

In 2005, the FWS [The U.S. Fish and Wildlife Service] allowed the import of over 17,000 sport-hunted trophies of CITES-listed species. The agency's policies and practices have consistently placed the interests of hunters over wildlife. The Safari Club International—the world's largest organization of trophy hunters—has influence and connections throughout the FWS that few other groups enjoy. And according to information recently obtained by the Animal Welfare Institute (AWI), these connections are now under investigation.

Animal Welfare Institute,
"Consumption First? Wildlife Trade Policy in the United States,"
AWI Quarterly, *vol. 56, no. 2, Spring 2007. www.awionline.com.*

Stricter Domestic Measures

One of the major obstacles limiting CITES' ability to support the sustainable use of biodiversity is its provision allowing stricter domestic measures (SDMs). This provision allows CITES Parties to unilaterally impose restrictions on wildlife trade that may be considerably stricter than those imposed by the Convention. SDMs have been a major source of conflict among CITES Parties since they may be used in ways that often diverge from CITES species conservation objectives. SDMs have been used to further political agendas, to discriminate in trading in order to benefit domestic constituencies, and to impose outside ethical values on developing countries. Although some Parties, and even the CITES Secretariat, have recently attempted to prohibit the use of SDMs, these efforts have been frustrated by the opposition of the United States and the European Union, among others.

In the United States, CITES is often superseded by the provisions of the Endangered Species Act (ESA), and by other domestic laws including the African Elephant Conservation Act, Eagle Protection Act, Marine Mammal Protection Act, Migratory Bird Treaty Act, Wild Bird Conservation Act, and Rhinoceros and Tiger Conservation Act. These acts impose stricter standards than CITES regarding the import of a number of Appendix II species. For example, the ESA imposes an "enhancement" standard for approving trade of Appendix II argali sheep, whereas the purpose of the CITES standard is only to show that trade will not be a "detriment" to the species' survival. Another example is the Namibian cheetah; the U.S. rejects its importation altogether, even though there are appropriate import quotas approved by CITES. Also, the import of the Nile crocodile was banned under the ESA for many years even when the species had been down-listed from Appendix I to Appendix II of CITES. . . . CITES should:

- Give guidance on stricter domestic measures in the form of *requirements*, not *recommendations*, to member nations.

- Require that plans to impose stricter domestic measures be announced at COP meetings, giving other member states the opportunity for debate and/or to be better prepared for the economic effects of a trade ban by another nation. . . .

Ranching and Captive Breeding

Given the potential benefits of ranching and captive breeding, there is a need for greater flexibility in CITES and the Endangered Species Act regarding the control over the creation of captive breeding and ranching facilities. Greater opportunities for experimentation would be desirable. Conditional approval of facilities for the purpose of testing an operation's impact on illegal trade, as well as benefits to wild populations, would be an important step in ascertaining the viability of such operations as conservation tools. If successful, captive breeding and ranching could prove valuable as a tool for preserving species, especially if used in conjunction with other methods of wildlife conservation. Certification of products raised in these facilities would enable consumers to purchase products raised in a sustainable manner. Under the proposal for an international wildlife royalty, as made elsewhere in this report, they would know that a portion of the price of the product may be returned to funding habitat and species conservation efforts in range states.

Thus, as one member of the SSC/IUCN Crocodile Specialist Group states, "while crocodilians are sometimes thought to be a rather special case in conservation and sustainable use, we argue that the general principles and experience derived within the context of the Convention for crocodilians has wide application for other organisms and the Convention in general." CITES should incorporate the applicable principles of sustainable use into future species listings as they may affect ranching and captive breeding. This chapter recommends that:

- Trade in ranched and captive-bred species should be permitted, thus enabling developing countries to utilize their resources, giving more value to both the animal and its habitat.

- There should be greater flexibility in transferring species from CITES Appendix I to Appendix II in order to facilitate ranching and captive breeding.

- CITES should establish education programs and eco-labeling in order to counter the image that all trade harms threatened and endangered species.

- CITES should include provisions for experiments to be conducted to assess the viability of ranching or captive breeding, including species commonly used to produce products for the traditional medicine trade. . . .

Genetic Rights to Wildlife

Concern for wildlife in the developed nations often does not translate into tangible economic benefits for the nations that are home to many important wildlife populations. Biodiversity has the quality of a "public good"; everyone may benefit, but there is inadequate incentive for any one party to provide the good in "socially optimal" amounts. However, if nations, or individuals, are able to profit directly from enhanced wildlife populations, there will likely be a much greater incentive for the conservation of biodiversity. The CBD has promoted this idea in the form of genetic property rights: sales of pharmaceuticals, pesticides, phytochemicals or cosmetics derived from plant resources of developing nations should be subject to royalty payments to the nation of the genetic material's origin. This idea is promising; corporations, such as Merck, Bristol-Myers Squibb, INDENA, Phytera, British Technology Group AMRAD, ICBG and Shaman, have voluntarily entered into financial agreements with Costa Rica and other biodiversity-rich Southern nations to develop natural resources. This funding has the potential to be substantial (in the many millions of dollars) and may prove to be a significant method to raise capital for conservation. . . .

Better Strategies Are Needed

Protection of the remaining rare and endangered wildlife is one of the most important tasks for the people of the world. This wildlife represents a priceless heritage whose loss would be a great human tragedy. Yet current strategies for protecting world wildlife are not working well. The developed nations state that they give a very high priority to preserving wildlife, but then expect developing nations—where most of the wildlife are located—to pay the largest burden of the costs. This discrepancy is fundamentally inequitable and cannot work as a long-term strategy for wildlife protection and preservation. Because of the ways in which it regulates international trade in endangered wildlife, CITES contributes to the imbalance between the nations that most strongly promote the conservation of endangered species and the nations that bear the majority of the costs of world wildlife preservation. CITES will only be effective when it genuinely works in concert with those national states that possess the majority of world wildlife, rather than against them.

> *"On average, candidate species have been waiting for protection for over 17 years. Clearly, species are experiencing substantial delays on the path to protection."*

More Species Should Be Declared Endangered

D. Noah Greenwald and Kieran F. Suckling

In this viewpoint, D. Noah Greenwald and Kieran F. Suckling argue that because the substantial protections of the Endangered Species Act (EPA) apply only to species that are officially listed as endangered or threatened, the logical first step is to list imperiled species without delay. In Greenwald and Suckling's analysis, however, the EPA listing process is badly flawed, subject to political interference, leaving candidate species waiting for protection for up to twenty-five years. Foot dragging has been egregious in the George W. Bush administration, they charge, with listings down to an average of seven per year, all court-ordered. The authors call for mandatory clearance of the backlog within five years and mandatory timelines for proposed species requiring a listing decision within two years. Conservation biologist D. Noah

D. Noah Greenwald and Kieran F. Suckling, "Progress or Extinction?: A Systematic Review of the U.S. Fish and Wildlife Service's Endangered Species Act Listing Program 1974–2004," Center for Biological Diversity, May 2005, pp. 3–10. Reproduced by permission.

*Greenwald oversees development of Endangered Species Act peti-
tions and Kieran F. Suckling is founder and policy director of the
Center for Biological Diversity, a nationwide conservation group
based in Tucson, Arizona, that monitors government and industry activity to ensure environmental laws are enforced and litigates on behalf of endangered species and habitats. Since its
founding in 1989, the Center has submitted proposals to put 225
species under ESA protection and won critical-habitat designation for 43 million acres.*

As you read, consider the following questions:

1. The ESA was amended in 1982 to include mandatory timelines for listing species. According to the
   authors, what loophole in this provision allows the
   U.S. executive branch to delay listing both high-
   priority and lower-priority species indefinitely?

2. As of 2005, how many plant and animal species are
   on the waiting list for Endangered Species Act protection, and what percentage of this number have
   been on the list for ten years or more, according to
   Greenwald and Suckling?

3. What three recommendations do the authors make
   to ensure that the current backlog of species can be
   listed within five years?

L isting of species as threatened or endangered has been
called the keystone of the U.S. Endangered Species Act
because it is only after species are listed that they receive the
substantial protections provided by the Act. Lengthy delays in
listing species known to warrant protection and political interference in listing of species have been persistent problems
in implementation of the listing program by the U.S. Fish and
Wildlife Service (FWS). The consequences of delayed protection are severe, allowing species to decline, making recovery

more costly and difficult, and in a number of cases resulting in species extinction. Indeed, at least 42 species have become extinct during a delay in the listing process.

In response to lack of progress in listing of imperiled species, Congress amended the Act in late 1982 to include mandatory timelines for listing species. Under these timelines, FWS is required to determine whether a species should be listed as threatened or endangered within two years of receiving a petition from a concerned citizen or organization. FWS was given one exception to this deadline. It may delay listing of lower priority species if it is making "expeditious progress" in listing higher-priority species. Congress emphasized, however, that the exception should not be used to justify the "foot-dragging efforts of a delinquent agency."

There are currently 286 plants and animals on the FWS waiting (i.e., candidate) list. Delaying protection of these species has been justified by the congressional exception, and thus can only be legal if expeditious progress is being made in processing the backlog of imperiled but unprotected species. On its face, the candidate list would suggest otherwise: 78 percent of the species (224) have been on the list for 10 or more years, [and] 26 percent (73) have been on the list for 25 or more years. On average, candidate species have been waiting for protection for over 17 years. Clearly, species are experiencing substantial delays on the path to protection.

What Constitutes "Expeditious Progress"?

To determine if FWS is making expeditious progress listing species under the Act, we determined the number of species listed per year [for the period] 1974–2004 by creating a detailed database of the listing history of all species listed under the Endangered Species Act. We obtained this information from an extensive search of the Federal Register. We further determined the number of listing determinations, both negative and positive, made by FWS from 1997 to 2004 based on an online database maintained by the agency. We calculated the number of listings per dollar from fiscal years 2000–2004 based on tables created by FWS of the cost of all listing findings during this period. To extend the record back in time, we compared the number of listings per dollar between 1997 and 1998 [as well as] 2002 to 2004 based on the congressional appropriation for listing. We did not include the years 1999– 2001, because spending on critical habitat and listing could not be separated during this period. During these two periods, we also compared the total number of determinations per dollar, because final listings are just one part of FWS' efforts to add species to the threatened and endangered list.

The Endangered Species Act does not specify how many species must be listed to qualify as expeditious progress. In 1990, however, the Inspector General of the Department of Interior audited the FWS endangered species program to determine if it conformed to the law and general standards of efficiency. In the two years prior to the review, FWS listed 46 species per year and promised it would list 50 species per year in the future. Based on the number of species on the candidate list at the time, the Inspector General concluded that a listing rate of 50 species per year would not constitute expeditious progress:

> Even if the Service meets its goals of listing 50 species per year, it will take 12 years to list the 601 candidate Category 1 species. In addition, based on Service staff estimates of candidate Category 2 species, it appears that approximately 1,300 to 1,800 of the 3,033 species now designated as candidate Category 2 species will eventually qualify for the Act's full protection. Again, even if the Service meets its goal of listing 50 species per year, it will take an additional 26 to 36 years to list those species currently classified as Category 2 candidates that may eventually need the Act's protection. Therefore, it may take from 38 to 48 years at current listing rates to list just those species now estimated to qualify for protection under the Act. In the meantime, additional spe-

cies will likely require the Act's protection. . . . We believe that this length of time to list and protect endangered species is not indicative of the 'expeditious progress' specified in the Act and could likely result in additional extinction of certain plants and animals during the period.

The Inspector General thus determined that listing of 50 species per year does not qualify as expeditious progress to the extent that it will not reduce the backlog within a timely manner.

Listing Has Slowed to a Near Halt

During the Nixon/Ford, Carter and Reagan administrations the agency averaged fewer [listings] than this, but it made progress toward the goal by developing an adequate infrastructure and steadily increasing the listing rate. During the [George H. W.] Bush Sr. and [Bill] Clinton administrations, the FWS averaged over 50 listings per year. That progress, however, has come to a near halt under the current [George W.] Bush administration. Between 2001 and 2004, the administration listed just 30 species, which translates into an average of seven per year. This is the fewest number of species and the lowest listing rate in any four-year period in the history of the Endangered Species Act. All of the listings, moreover, were under court order. It is the only administration to make no listings of its own accord.

The current administration's annual listing rate is also considerably lower than the 45 species per year listed between 1974 and 2000. The only comparably low period was 1981–1982 following the election of Ronald Reagan and the appointment of James Watt as Secretary of the Interior. This period of few listings prompted Congress to amend the Endangered Species Act in 1982 to include mandatory listing timelines.

Currently, there are 286 species on the candidate list; 27 more than contained in the 2001 list. If FWS maintains its

Hundreds of Endangered Species Languish on the Waiting List

The U.S. Fish and Wildlife Service has already declared that 225 plants and animals qualify as proposed endangered species. Instead of protecting them, however, it has placed them on a waiting list called the "candidate list." A [2007] report by the Center for Biological Diversity shows that systematic delays, including lengthy waits on the candidate list, contributed to the extinction of 83 species between 1974 and 1994.

Seventy-nine percent of the 225 species (178) have been on the candidate for at least ten years, 38% percent (86) have waited at least 20 years, and 28% (64) have been waiting since 1975. On average, the 225 species have been on the waiting list for 17 years. . . .

"It is too late to save the California grizzly bear, the eastern cougar, the Carolina parakeet, the passenger pigeon, or the silver trout. They became extinct before America created the Endangered Species Act, our modern day Noah's Ark," said Dr. [Robert] Hass. "But we're not too late to save the 225 plants and animals languishing on the federal candidate list. It's time to open the doors of the ark and let them in. They should be placed on the endangered species list as soon as possible."

Center for Biological Diversity, Scientists, Artists, and Conservationists Petition Bush Administration to Place 225 Plants and Animals on Endangered List, *May 4, 2004. www.biologicaldiversity.org.*

current rate of listing seven species per year, it will take 41 years to list these 286 species, by which time many others will have been found to similarly require protection and have been added to the candidate species list. This length of time is longer than that determined by the Inspector General in 1990 to not be expeditious progress.

Listing of species involves a series of determinations that are published in the Federal Register. Upon receipt of a petition, FWS first issues a finding determining whether the petition presents sufficient information to warrant further consideration. If the determination is positive, FWS has 12 months from the date of the petition to conduct a status review and either propose to list the species, determine listing is not warranted, or designate the species warranted but precluded. If the species is proposed, FWS has 12 months to finalize or withdraw listing.

FWS can also initiate listing by either making a species a candidate, in which case there is no timeline, or simply issuing a proposed rule, requiring them to issue a final rule in 12 months. All of these determinations arguably constitute progress towards listing species as threatened and endangered.

Negative Decisions Have Quadrupled

Even if all determinations are considered, the Bush administration is still making far less progress towards listing species. FWS issued far fewer listing determinations and a greater proportion of negative determinations from 2001 to 2004 than in the previous four years (1997–2000). From 1997 to 2000, FWS issued a total of 375 listing determinations, for an average of 94 determinations per year, resulting in listing of 192 species. Of these determinations, only 12 percent were negative listing decisions. From 2001 to 2004, in contrast, FWS issued a total of only 94 determinations, for a rate of 24 per year, 48 percent of which have been negative findings.

A quadrupling in the rate of negative findings is reflective of the administration's stated opposition to protecting species under the Endangered Species Act. Indeed, a number of the negative determinations were reversals of past warranted determinations (e.g., coastal cutthroat trout) or were found to be illegal (e.g., green sturgeon and Yellowstone cutthroat trout). A survey of FWS biologists conducted by the Union of Concerned Scientists indicates that administration officials are intervening in endangered species decisions. The survey found that nearly half of all respondents whose work is related to endangered species scientific findings (44 percent) reported that they "have been directed, for non-scientific reasons, to refrain from making jeopardy or other findings that are protective of species."

All 30 species listed under the Bush administration followed court orders forcing the FWS to make a determination, making this administration the only one to not list any species at its own discretion. Indeed, the administration has made very few determinations without court order, particularly when compared to the Clinton administration. During the second term of the Clinton Administration, FWS made 390 listing determinations, of which 188 (48 percent) were non-court ordered. In contrast, during the first term of the Bush administration, FWS only made 98 listing determinations, only 6 (6 percent) of which were non-court ordered.

FWS claims that expeditious progress is a function of whether or not they are using available funding efficiently, stating that expeditious progress "is a function of the resources that are available and the way in which those resources are used." Even accepting the argument that expeditious progress is determined by the efficient use of funding, FWS is not making such progress. FWS argues that it is listing fewer species because the listing budget has been captured by court-ordered critical habitat designations. To determine if FWS is efficiently using its funds specifically allocated for listing and thus is making expeditious progress according to the agency's own measure, we examined two documents produced by FWS that provide an estimate of the costs of the majority of individual listing findings—both court ordered and non-court ordered—made for fiscal years 2000–2004.

Insufficient Funding Is Not the Problem

According to FWS' figures, during 2000, FWS spent $1.62 million making listing determinations and listed 36 species for a rate of nearly 22 species per million dollars. From 2001 to 2004, however, FWS only listed an average of seven species per million dollars, including listing only two species per million dollars in 2003 and six species per million dollars in 2004.

Further evidence of a drop in the number of listings per dollar spent after 2000 is provided by comparing the number of species listed per million dollars in fiscal years 1997 and 1998 with fiscal years 2002–2004. We chose 1997 and 1998 because FWS proposed critical habitat for only one species in each year and finalized critical habitat for only one species in 1997 and only three species in 1998, meaning that it can be conservatively assumed that the majority of the listing/critical habitat budget was spent on listing determinations. Beginning in 2002, Congress created a budgetary subcap limiting spending for critical habitat designation to a fixed amount. As a result, it is possible to determine how much money FWS specifically had for listing independent of critical habitat.

Similar to the results above, the number of species listed per million dollars was far less in fiscal years 2002–2004 compared to 1997 and 1998. In 1997, FWS listed 30 species per million dollars. This rate was lower in 1998, but not nearly so low as 2003 and 2004. Had FWS maintained a listing rate of 30 species per million dollars, it would have listed as many as 270 species during 2002–2004 based on an annual listing budget of $3 million. Even had they maintained a listing rate of seven species per million dollars, as they did in 1998, FWS would have listed 63 species during 2002–2004, compared to the 26 species that it actually listed.

Not only did FWS issue large numbers of final rules listing species, they also issued a large number of total determinations. Comparing the total number of listing determinations, including 90-day findings, 12-month findings and final listing determinations, between fiscal years 1997–1998 and fiscal years 2002–2004, it is clear that FWS made far fewer listing determinations per million dollars in 2002–2004 than in 1997–1998.

The above data show that FWS has made fewer total determinations and has listed fewer species per dollar since 2001, demonstrating that FWS is not efficiently using available funds to make expeditious progress.

How Are Species Listed?

Mandatory timelines for listing enacted in 1982 created two processes by which species are listed as threatened or endangered. In the first, listing is initiated by petition from a citizen or organization and the agency is required to determine whether listing is warranted within two years. In the second, listing is initiated at the agency's discretion and there is no fixed deadline by which a listing determination must be made.

The mandatory timelines significantly speeded listing, reducing delays in listing from 14 to four years and resulting in petitioned species being listed in less time than species listed at the agencies' discretion. Citizen enforcement of the timelines through lawsuits also reduced listing delays, decreasing time to proposed rule from seven to 2.4 years and from proposed to final rule from 1.4 to 0.7 years.

The timelines and citizen enforcement also increased the rate of species listings. From 1974–1982, the agencies listed an average of 23 species per year. From 1983–1990, following enactment of the timelines, the agencies listed an average of 40 species per year. Although [this represented] an increase in the listing rate, many species continued to languish without protection. In response, conservation groups began actively working to enforce the timelines through litigation, resulting in a significant increase in the rate of species listings to 73 per year from 1991 to 1995.

Summary & Recommendations

[Since 2001], FWS listed the fewest total number of species in the history of the Endangered Species Act, and the fewest species per dollar spent. These factors demonstrate that FWS is not making expeditious progress towards listing species known to require protection and that have been awaiting ESA protection for an average of 17 years. This has resulted in an increase in the backlog of candidate species, which will continue to grow under the current listing rate. Candidate species receive no protection under the Act, nor are they covered by the mandatory timelines for petitioned species and thus are at risk of extinction. The following actions are necessary to alleviate this situation:

1. Create a "Listing SWAT Team" to complete listing proposals for the 286 candidate species within the next five years.

2. To ensure listing of the 286 species is completed in five years, identify taxonomically related species or species from the same ecosystem for inclusion in multi-species listing rules.

3. To expedite the existing peer review process, fund the National Academy of Sciences to form a committee to peer review proposed rules for the 286 species.

4. Increase the annual listing budget to $25 million to ensure FWS does not again develop a backlog.

5. Enact mandatory timelines for candidate species requiring listing within two years.

> "[P]aradoxically, declaring a species endangered may make it more desirable and thereby increase the likelihood of exploitation."

Declaring a Species Endangered Actually Hastens Its Decline

Franck Courchamp et al.

In this viewpoint, French researcher Franck Courchamp and his colleagues at the National Center for Scientific Research of the University of Paris-Sud argue that the official declaration of a species as endangered or threatened by the Convention on International Trade in Endangered Species (CITES) or the Endangered Species Act (ESA) paradoxically increases its risk of extinction. The authors call this the anthropogenic allee effect, or AAE: A species' appearance on a CITES or ESA list is proof that it is rare, rarity increases its value, and the rarer it is the more it is in demand (at any price) by collectors, trophy hunters, luxury food consumers, exotic pet traders, ecotourists, and traditional medicine practitioners. Courchamp et al. offer evidence that the

AEE has driven many species to near-extinction, and urge legislators and environmentalists not *to declare a species endangered if it cannot then be fully protected.*

As you read, consider the following questions:

1. According to Courchamp et al., how does the allee effect threaten the survival of endangered Papua New Guinea butterflies?

2. How do the authors suggest mere descriptions of the turtle *C. mccordi* and the gecko *G. luii* in the scientific literature further harmed these species?

3. Why do the authors consider ecotourism a human activity that potentially triggers an allee effect?

Overexploitation of living species (i.e., human exploitation exceeding the species' regeneration capacity) is a major threat to biodiversity, yet theory predicts that economic extinction (exploitation cessation) will usually precede ecological extinction (population disappearance). As populations become more sparse, it is increasingly costly to exploit them, and exploitation ceases to be beneficial. In the absence of natural extinction risks at low population size (e.g., demographic [variability]), exploitation cessation allows for the species' recovery.

However, less-abundant species could suffer disproportionately from exploitation if their rarity makes them systematically more valuable. We postulate that because rarity makes living species attractive, their (over) exploitation can remain profitable, rendering such species even rarer, and driving them to extinction.

Defining the AAE

This human-generated feedback loop is very similar to the Allee effect, an important process in basic ecology and applied conservation biology. . . . In many animal and plant species, individual reproduction and survival is diminished in small populations through various mechanisms, including mate shortage, failure to optimize the environment, or lack of conspecific cooperation. Populations suffering from Allee effects may exhibit negative growth rates at low densities, which drives them to even lower densities and ultimately to extinction. A typical example is that of obligate cooperative breeding species, which need group members to enable them to raise offspring, survive predators, and/or forage cooperatively, and fail to do so efficiently when their numbers drop.

Although studies on Allee effects are continuing, it has been generally accepted that the Allee effect is intrinsic to the species concerned, which express it naturally at low density. Therefore, human activities cannot create an Allee effect; at most, they can push species into density ranges where their natural Allee effect will be expressed. On the contrary, we show here that humans can induce a purely artificial Allee effect in rare species through the "paradox of value." We call it the anthropogenic Allee effect (AAE). Although familiar to economists, the paradox of value—also called the "water and diamonds paradox" (water has much value in use but none in exchange, while the opposite is true for diamonds)—is absent from ecological theory. [We propose that] an AAE can, in theory, emerge in wildlife-related trade as soon as rarity acquires value. We then identify a number of human activities where an AAE can occur and use examples to illustrate each of them.

Two Fundamental Assumptions

The AAE is founded on two fundamental assumptions: (i) there is a positive correlation between species rarity and its value, and (ii) this correlation fuels sufficient demand to ensure that the market price exceeds the escalating costs of finding and harvesting a declining species. If these simple conditions are met, harvesting reduces the population of the rare species, increasing its rarity and therefore its value, which stimulates further harvesting and drives the species into an extinction vortex. . . .

Data showing a positive relationship between price and rarity are scarce but do exist for a number of nature-related economic activities. The second assumption of the AAE, that prices increase with rarity faster than the exploitation costs, may be more difficult to test. In general, one might expect that increasing exploitation costs lead to increasing prices, which in turn results in a drop in demand. However, other factors act to reinforce the demand, for example, when it becomes fashionable to acquire a rare item. The second assumption is therefore fulfilled if there are always a few consumers willing to acquire the last individuals at any price. In this case, ecological extinction (the end of the species) will precede economic extinction (cessation of exploitation). . . .

We claim that a number of human activities can create an AAE. Below, we develop some examples that illustrate under what conditions people are willing to pay (or risk) substantial amounts for the satisfaction and/or prestige of acquiring rare species. . . .

Collections

The most straightforward example of a nature-related activity where rarity is valued is that of hobby collections, where the rarest items are the most valued and thus demand the highest prices. As the value of a rare item increases, more time, effort, or resources may be devoted to trying to acquire it, increasing the pressure on the species as it becomes rarer. The collection of butterflies in Papua New Guinea illustrates this point, whereby the price of butterflies sold by villagers to insect collectors were correlated with rarity, even when corrected by size. Therefore, it is the rarity of the butterflies, not their size, that drives the price of these collection items. Collectors of wildlife items such as other insects, bird eggs, mollusk shells, or orchids often adhere to this rule. For example, the collection of bird eggs threatens many rare species in the United Kingdom, and this practice continues despite the threat of financial penalties and/or jail terms. When species are protected by local laws and/or by international trade treaties, the high price that the rarest species can fetch on the collection market is a powerful incentive to poachers and smugglers to seek and illegally sell the most expensive (rare) species, constituting a real threat to some of these species.

Scientists have historically been, and in some cases still are, among these enthusiastic collectors of natural specimens. Following the overexploitation of the great auk *Pinguinus impennis* for food and feathers, the species became very rare. As a consequence, these birds became a valuable item for collectors—among them, ornithologists and museum administrators, who were eager to acquire eggs or skins of the rare and soon to be extinct bird, thereby precipitating its extinction. The great auk provides a possible example of an AAE leading to a species extinction and should serve as a warning for currently threatened species.

Trophy Hunting

Trophy hunting represents another form of collection. For thousands of years, several cultures have valued trophies as a sign of manhood and virility. Species that were difficult to kill symbolized power, because power was required to kill them. However, because sophisticated firearms are now used, the emphasis of hunting has shifted from dangerous to rare animals. Rarer species are harder to find, so greater hunting skill—and greater wealth—is required, and greater prestige is gained by killing them. We compared the standardised quality of trophies of 57 species and subspecies of *Caprinae* [goat antelopes] hunted for their trophies with the average price of the trophy hunting in the 2006 season, as proposed by various hunting tour operators on the Internet. . . . Once again, our results show that hunting trophy prices are correlated with rarity, regardless of size: the rarer the trophy, the more valuable and expensive it is. For wild sheep alone, wealthy hunters are willing to pay more than US$400,000 at auctions to shoot a rare animal, because few of their peers will be able to do so, and they will gain social prestige in being one of the few who can afford it. Very few hunting permits are delivered for protected species, making the animals even more attractive to trophy collectors and possibly stimulating illegal hunting.

Luxury Items

The consumption of rare species as luxury food items is another way of displaying wealth and/or social status. The rarer the item, the more expensive it is, and the more prestige is gained by its acquisition. When closing deals, wealthy Asian businessmen wishing to display their affluence will pay large amounts of money to eat a plate of lips of a large Napoleon wrasse, *Cheilinus undulatus* (a single pair of lips costs US$250). By the mid 1990s, Napoleon wrasse became the most sought-after reef fish in the world, and is currently number one on the "top ten most-wanted species" list published by the World Wide Fund for Nature. Populations in South East Asia are now extinct on many reefs, and very few large individuals survive in the remaining fragmented populations. The caviar obtained from different sturgeon species provides another example for the potential for the feedback loop we describe here. Not only are all sturgeon species currently on the IUCN Red List and CITES Appendices, but the price of the caviar is correlated with its rarity. Abalones, of which six species suffer from overfishing on the Pacific coast of North America, are another illustration. Considered a delicacy in California, white abalones, the rarest of the six abalone species, have declined by over 99.99% due to increasing overfishing, in part illegal (the fishery was closed in 1996), while at the same time, prices have escalated. Even taking fishing effort into account, the vol-

159

ume of abalones fished is inversely proportional to the price. Although white abalones were the first marine invertebrate on the United States endangered species list in 2001, this species could become extinct within a decade unless extraordinary recovery measures are implemented. Due to the demand for other types of luxury items, such as exotic woods, furs, turtle shells, or snake and crocodile skins, many other species are likely to be vulnerable to AAEs in this context.

Exotic Pets

Another activity that can lead to an AAE is exotic pet ownership, which is an increasingly important part of the wildlife trade business. Reptile, bird, monkey, and felid [wild cat] pets are becoming ever more fashionable in some parts of the world, with the rarest species being especially sought after. Given that high levels of mortality occur during the capture or transfer of traded species due to inadequacies in care, the massive volumes of live species that are traded are likely to exert considerable pressure on the target populations. Unlike the trophy hunting market, the exotic pet market involves many taxa, including arachnids, molluscs, insects, fish, and other vertebrates. For example, aquarium "hardcore" collectors seek rare items such as the peppermint angelfish *Centropyge boylei*, which sell for over US$10,000. Even though the trade of many such animals is illegal, smugglers generally face low penalties and therefore continue to deplete endangered populations for large amounts of money.

A recent article reports that immediately after being described in the scientific literature, the turtle *Chelodina mccordi* from the small Indonesian island of Roti and the gecko *Goniurosaurus luii* from southeastern China became recognized as rarities in the international pet trade, and prices in importing countries soared to highs of US$1,500 to US$2,000 each.

Collectors Target the Rarest Species

The shady pursuit of endangered bird eggs made international headlines in May 2006 when Colin Watson, widely considered Britain's most notorious illegal egg collector, died after falling from a 12-meter tree, allegedly while hunting a rare egg. (Watson's son Kevin has publicly claimed that his father hadn't collected an egg since the practice was banned in 1985.) The Royal Society for the Protection of Birds estimates that up to 30 of Britain's most vulnerable species are targeted by collectors. . . .

As long as there is a positive correlation between a species' rarity and its value, and the market price exceeds the cost of harvesting the species, harvesting will cause further declines, making the species ever rarer and more expensive, which in turn stimulates even more harvesting until there's nothing left to harvest.

Liza Gross, "A Human Taste for Rarity Spells Disaster for Endangered Species," PloS Biology, vol. 4, no. 12, November 28, 2006. http://biology.plosjournal.org.

They became so heavily hunted that today, *C. mccordi* is nearly extinct in the wild and *G. luii* is extirpated from its type locality.

Some individuals in the wildlife trade business believe that the declaration of a species as endangered by a conservation organization provides official proof that the species is rare and therefore more valuable. Hence, paradoxically, declaring a species endangered may make it more desirable and thereby increase the likelihood of exploitation. We compared the selling prices of exotic amphibian and reptile species sold as pets in early 2006 by the largest herpetologist retailer in France (which sells to the other retailers in Europe as well as to the public) according to the CITES status of the species. When corrected by adult weight, species that have a CITES status were found to be significantly more expensive than species with no CITES status, probably as a consequence of their being considered more valuable as a result of their rarity.

To further investigate the effect of CITES status on perceived value of the species, we analyzed the CITES database to assess the effect on illegal trade of a change of status, for species passing from Appendix 2 (species whose survival might be compromised if trade was not restricted) to Appendix 1 (very restricted trade, species threatened with extinction, perceived as the rarest). Of the 133 plant and animal species that have undergone this change over the past 30 years, 44 have never been reported as being traded illegally. Interestingly, classification of some species as highly endangered resulted in an increase in their illegal trade: Of the 89 remaining species, 23 (25.8%) have shown a marked peak of illegal trade during the period corresponding to the change in CITES status (because the change is officially proposed 9–15 months before the application, poachers can be informed one full year in advance). This is a compelling illustration of both the increased attractiveness of rarer species and the exacerbated threat this classification may have on species becoming rare if they cannot be properly protected.

Ecotourism

Ecotourism ventures have expanded greatly in recent years, with the public increasingly wanting to experience a closeness to natural ecosystems or species. Such activities often involve encountering and/or observing rare species. Given that some ecotourism activities have been shown to generate disturbances that are detrimental to the fitness of observed species, we can assume that rare species, especially those that are charismatic, will be disproportionately impacted upon by ecotourism. Consequently, activities such as observing rare birds, whales, primates, or nesting sea turtles have the potential to generate an AAE, especially when the animals are globally rare but with reliable sightings locally. For example, D. E. Bain studied the relationships between the number of killer whales *Orcinus orca* in the Southern resident population (eastern North Pacific) and the number of boats registered for conducting killer whale watching tours. He found a significant inverse relationship between the number of boats observed in one year with the whale population size recorded the subsequent year. Motorized boats are known to cause disturbances to whales and lower their fitness. More interestingly, there was also an inverse relationship between the decreasing whale population size recorded during one year, and the increasing size of the boat fleet the next year, indicating that contrary to expected economics, the increasing rarity of that population of killer whales did not immediately stop whale watching but may have in fact stimulated it. In 2001, the number of boats in the commercial whale watching fleet exceeded the number of killer whales in the population.

The Capercaillie (*Tetrao urogallus*) is a large gamebird that inhabits Scottish forests, where its population has dropped precipitously from 20,000 to 900 birds in the past 30 years. Mating takes place just a few times each spring at the display grounds, or leks, of the males. Given the rarity of these birds, there is great interest in observing these leks amongst British birdwatchers, and disturbance of leks is thought to be a serious threat to the survival of the Scottish population.

Traditional Medicine

Traditional medicine uses many rare and endangered species. Although other aspects may influence ingredient choice, rarity certainly plays a role and may therefore result in an AAE. In western Japan, the red morph of *Geranium thunbergii*, a flower widely used for treating stomach problems and diarrhea, is common, whereas the white morph is rare. The morph frequency is the opposite in eastern Japan, with the white morph being common and the red morph rare. People in western Japan believe that the medicinal efficiency of the "rare" white morph is better, whereas those in eastern Japan consider the "rare" red morph superior. This geographic difference in people's beliefs is likely to exert strong selective pressure on flower colour and offers a good illustration of the preference for rarity and its perceived medicinal virtues.

The Chinese bahaba *Bahaba taipingensis* provides another example of the effect that exploitation for traditional medicine can have on rare populations. Used for the prevention of miscarriages, the swimbladder of this fish is highly valued in Asia; as indicated by the name "soft gold", which was assigned to it by fishers as it became increasingly rare over the last four decades. As the exploitation of this fish intensified, its increasing rarity made its value escalate to such a level that despite less than half a dozen fish being caught per year in the 1990s (less than 1% of the amount caught in the 1960s), 100–200 boats continued to target this fish. One large swimbladder was sold in the 1980s for US$64,000. In 2001, some 70 years after it was first reported in the scientific literature, this species was virtually extinct. At that time, the occasional fish that was caught every few years yielded a swimbladder with a value that on the top retail market, weight for weight, exceeded that of gold by seven times.

Conclusion

We have identified six different types of human activities that have the potential to induce an AAE, but there are likely to be others. It is important to realize that an AAE has the potential to target not only the most charismatic and emblematic species, but also the most inconspicuous invertebrate, as long as rarity renders it fashionable to exploit for one reason or another. Furthermore, species that are currently not of concern could very well be in the near future.

Because among the activities presented here several are primarily stimulated by people interested in nature, it is important that these people are aware of and have an understanding of the potential effect their actions may have on the very species they appreciate. Consequently, informing potential ecotourists, collectors, and pet owners may in part facilitate the process of reducing the likelihood of an AAE and thus the impact on the species that are the targets of these activities. However, activities that relate to prestige or tradition may require more dramatic actions—including strengthened regulations and targeted, adapted information—to decrease the likelihood of AAEs in the target species.

How the trade of rare species should be regulated is a vast and ongoing debate. The finding that rarity itself could be a criterion for immediate threat to a species because of the psychological and economic value people attach to it is, however, a new and important piece of information in the battle to preserve biodiversity. At the very least, this finding should lead to the realization that declaring a species too rare to be subjected to legal transactions could be dangerous for the species if it cannot be fully protected. At most, it is hoped that such information could change our rationale on the manner in which biodiversity is perceived and exploited.

Periodical Bibliography

The following articles have been selected to supplement the diverse views presented in this chapter.

Raluca Albu — "Wolf Pact," *OnEarth*, vol. 29, no. 2, Summer 2007.

Sharon Begley — "Cry of the Wild," *Newsweek*, August 6, 2007.

Economist — "Trading Down: In Preserving Rare Species, Less May Be More," June 2, 2007.

Catherine Fairweather — "Seeing (and Saving) the Tiger: Catching a Glimpse of an Elusive Bengal Tiger Isn't the Only Draw for Visitors to India's Ranthambore National Park," *Town & Country*, June 2007.

International Fund for Animal Welfare — *Bidding for Extinction: Wildlife Trade on the Web*, 2007. www.ifaw.org.

Scott Johnson — "Gorilla Warfare," *Newsweek*, August 6, 2007.

Joe Kerkvliet and Christian Langpap — "Learning from Endangered and Threatened Species Recovery Programs: A Case Study Using U.S. Endangered Species Act Recovery Scores," *Ecological Economics*, August 1, 2007.

Timothy D. Male — "A Closer Look at the Endangered Species Act," *BioScience*, July–August 2007.

Helen O'Neill — "How Smuggler of Endangered Butterflies Was Finally Netted," *San Jose Mercury-News*, August 18, 2007.

Science Daily — "CITES Updates Wildlife Trade Rules," June 18, 2007.

TTJ: The Timber Industry Magazine — "CITES No Solution for Protection," June 23, 2007.

Martin Varley — "Conventional Weapons," *Geographical*, vol. 79, no. 6, June 2007.

OPPOSING
VIEWPOINTS®
SERIES

CHAPTER 4

How Should Humans Respond to Species Decline?

Chapter Preface

The question of whether the biome can withstand or recover from significant biodiversity loss involves many complex issues—habitat destruction, species extinction, resource depletion, pollution, population growth—but every consideration of the question rests on two premises: 1) humankind is by far the dominant species on Earth, and 2) human interests and the interests of much of the rest of the world's flora and fauna are not easily reconciled. In October 2006, *New Scientist* magazine published an article that considered the question from an intriguing alternative theoretical perspective: Would biodiversity recover if humans disappeared?

The answer, Bob Holmes writes in "Imagine Earth Without People," is yes, and sooner than you think. In his "thought experiment," Holmes proposes a scenario in which the world's human population of 6.5 billion is instantly transported to a far-off galaxy. According to British civil engineer Gordon Masterton, the lights will go out within 48 hours, ending light pollution. Automobile-exhaust and smokestack pollution will be filtered out of the atmosphere in a year, chlorofluorocarbons within a few decades, methane within a hundred years. Excess nitrates and phosphates will clear out of freshwater bodies in a few decades and overfished ocean species will gradually recover in the same time span, Buildings, bridges, and dams will crumble within 250 years, though their ruins may be visible for several thousand years longer. Biodiversity, especially in warm, moist regions, will begin to recover within a few decades, based on the real-world example of the evacuated region surrounding the Chernobyl nuclear accident:

> In the absence of human activity, the forest will close over 80 percent of [areas still rich in native species] within 50 years, and all but 5 percent within 200. . . . Feral descen-

dants of domesticated animals and plants are likely to become permanent additions in many ecosystems. . . . Biologists estimate that habitat loss is pivotal in about 85 percent of cases where U.S. species become endangered, so most such species will benefit once habitats begin to rebound. However, species in the direst straits may have already passed some critical threshold below which they lack the genetic diversity . . . to recover. These "dead species walking"—cheetahs and California condors, for example—are likely to slip away regardless.

According to atmospheric chemist Susan Solomon, carbon dioxide will be the longest-lasting legacy of human existence: It may take 20,000 years for the oceans to absorb the atmospheric excess. A related study by University of California-Berkeley paleontologists estimates that it would take around 10 million years for biodiversity to reach pre-human levels, but obvious signs of the existence of an advanced civilization will have disappeared long before that, in less than 100,000 years. Earth, Holmes concludes, will quickly forget human beings.

The viewpoints in this chapter stick to reality in tackling the issue of how to respond to species decline, a problem for which there are no easy answers and, some experts argue, there is little time for wishful thinking.

> *"[R]ewilding is not about recreating exactly some past state. Rather it is about restoring the kinds of species interactions that sustain thriving ecosystems."*

Rewilding North America Is a Good Conservation Strategy

C. Josh Donlan

In this viewpoint, ecologist C. Josh Donlan advocates a radical plan called Pleistocene rewilding to prevent the extinction of the world's wild large vertebrate species, or megafauna. Pleistocene rewilding is the phased introduction into North America of animals descended from species (such as mammoths) that once existed there but went extinct 13,000 years ago. According to Donlan, with proper management large animals such as wild horses, camels, cheetahs, Asian and African elephants, lions, and giant tortoises can be safely restocked in North America. He maintains that the ecological, evolutionary, economic, aesthetic, educational, and ethical benefits of his rewilding plan outweigh its costs and risks. C. Josh Donlan is a research biologist at Cornell University, where he earned a Ph.D. in ecology and evolutionary biology. He is the founder and director of Advanced Conserva-

tion Strategies, a nongovernmental organization dedicated to restoring ecosystems and halting extinctions. Donlan is also an advisor to the Galapagos National Park and the group Island Conservation.

As you read, consider the following questions:

1. According to Donlan, what large-mammal species once thrived in North America and why did they go extinct?
2. How does the author propose to protect people from introduced predator species?
3. How does the reintroduction of gray wolves to Yellowstone National Park serve as an example of how rewilding works, according to Donlan?

In the fall of 2004 a dozen conservation biologists gathered on a ranch in New Mexico to ponder a bold plan. The scientists, trained in a variety of disciplines, ranged from the grand old men of the field to those of us earlier in our careers. The idea we were mulling over was the reintroduction of large vertebrates—megafauna—to North America.

Most of these animals, such as mammoths and cheetahs, died out roughly 13,000 years ago, when humans from Eurasia began migrating to the continent. The theory—propounded 40 years ago by Paul Martin of the University of Arizona—is that overhunting by the new arrivals reduced the numbers of large vertebrates so severely that the populations could not recover. Called Pleistocene overkill, the concept was highly controversial at the time, but the general thesis that humans played a significant role is now widely accepted. Martin was present at the meeting in New Mexico, and his ideas on the loss of these animals, the ecological consequences, and what we should do about it formed the foundation of the proposal that emerged, which we dubbed Pleistocene rewilding.

Athough the cheetahs, lions and mammoths that once roamed North America are extinct, the same species or close relatives have survived elsewhere, and our discussions focused on introducing these substitutes to North American ecosystems. We believe that these efforts hold the potential to partially restore important ecological processes, such as predation and browsing, to ecosystems where they have been absent for millennia. The substitutes would also bring economic and cultural benefits. Not surprisingly, the published proposal evoked strong reactions. Those reactions are welcome, because debate about the conservation issues that underlie Pleistocene rewilding merit thorough discussion.

Why Big Animals Are Important

Our approach concentrates on large animals because they exercise a disproportionate effect on the environment. For tens of millions of years, megafauna dominated the globe, strongly interacting and co-evolving with other species and influencing entire ecosystems. Horses, camels, lions, elephants and other large creatures were everywhere: Megafauna were the norm. But starting roughly 50,000 years ago, the overwhelming majority went extinct. Today megafauna inhabit less than 10 percent of the globe.

Over the past decade, ecologist John Terborgh of Duke University has observed directly how critical large animals are to the health of ecosystems and how their loss adversely affects the natural world. When a hydroelectric dam flooded thousands of acres in Venezuela, Terborgh saw the water create dozens of islands—a fragmentation akin to the virtual islands created around the world as humans cut down trees, build shopping malls, and sprawl from urban centers. The islands in Venezuela were too small to support the creatures at the top of the food chain—predators such as jaguars, pumas and eagles. Their disappearance sparked a chain of reactions. Animals such as monkeys, leaf-cutter ants and other herbivores, whose populations were no longer kept in check by predation, thrived and subsequently destroyed vegetation—the ecosystems collapsed, with biodiversity being the ultimate loser.

Similar ecological disasters have occurred on other continents. Degraded ecosystems are not only bad for biodiversity; they are bad for human economies. In Central America, for instance, researchers have shown that intact tropical ecosystems are worth at least $60,000 a year to a single coffee farm because of the services they provide, such as the pollination of coffee crops.

Where large predators and herbivores still remain, they play pivotal roles. In Alaska, sea otters maintain kelp forest ecosystems by keeping herbivores that eat kelp, such as sea urchins, in check. In Africa, elephants are keystone players; as they move through an area, their knocking down trees and trampling create a habitat in which certain plants and animals can flourish. Lions and other predators control the populations of African herbivores, which in turn influence the distribution of plants and soil nutrients.

In Pleistocene America, large predators and herbivores played similar roles. Today most of that vital influence is absent. For example, the American cheetah (a relative of the African cheetah) dashed across the grasslands in pursuit of pronghorn antelopes for millions of years. These chases shaped the pronghorn's astounding speed and other biological aspects of one of the fastest animals alive. In the absence of the cheetah, the pronghorn appears "overbuilt" for its environment today.

Pleistocene rewilding is not about recreating exactly some past state. Rather it is about restoring the kinds of species interactions that sustain thriving ecosystems. Giant tortoises, horses, camels, cheetahs, elephants and lions: They were all here, and they helped to shape North American ecosystems. Either the same species or closely related species are available for introduction as proxies, and many are already in captivity

173

in the U.S. In essence, Pleistocene rewilding would help change the underlying premise of conservation biology from limiting extinction to actively restoring natural processes.

At first, our proposal may seem outrageous—lions in Montana? But the plan deserves serious debate for several reasons. First, nowhere on Earth is pristine, at least in terms of being substantially free of human influence. Our demographics, chemicals, economics and politics pervade every part of the planet. Even in our largest national parks, species go extinct without active intervention. And human encroachment shows alarming signs of worsening. Bold actions, rather than business as usual, will be needed to reverse such negative influences. Second, since conservation biology emerged as a discipline more than three decades ago, it has been mainly a business of doom and gloom, a struggle merely to slow the loss of biodiversity. But conservation need not be only reactive. A proactive approach would include restoring natural processes, starting with ones we know are disproportionately important, such as those influenced by megafauna.

Third, land in North America is available for the reintroduction of megafauna. Although the patterns of human land use are always shifting, in some areas, such as parts of the Great Plains and the Southwest, large private and public lands with low or declining human population densities might be used for the project. Fourth, bringing megafauna back to America would also bring tourist and other dollars into nearby communities and enhance the public's appreciation of the natural world. More than 1.5 million people visit San Diego's Wild Animal Park every year to catch a glimpse of large mammals. Only a handful of U.S. national parks receive that many visitors. Last, the loss of some of the remaining species of megafauna in Africa and Asia within this century seems likely—Pleistocene rewilding could help reverse that.

How It Might Be Done

We are not talking about backing up a van and kicking some cheetahs out into your backyard. Nor are we talking about doing it tomorrow. We conceive of Pleistocene rewilding as a series of staged, carefully managed ecosystem manipulations. What we are offering here is a vision—not a blueprint—of how this might be accomplished. And by no means are we suggesting that rewilding should be a priority over current conservation programs in North America or Africa. Pleistocene rewilding could proceed alongside such conservation efforts, and it would likely generate conservation dollars from new funding sources, rather than competing for funds with existing conservation efforts.

The long-term vision includes a vast, securely fenced ecological history park, encompassing thousands of square miles, where horses, camels, elephants and large carnivores would roam. As happens now in Africa and regions surrounding some U.S. national parks, the ecological history park would not only attract ecotourists but would also provide jobs related both to park management and to tourism.

To get to that distant point, we would need to start modestly, with relatively small-scale experiments that assess the impacts of megafauna on North American landscapes. These controlled experiments, guided by sound science and by the fossil record, which indicates what animals actually lived here, could occur first on donated or purchased private lands and could begin immediately. They will be critical in answering the many questions about the reintroductions and would help lay out the costs and benefits of rewilding.

One of these experiments is already under way. Spurred by our 2004 meeting, biologists recently reintroduced Bolson tortoises to a private ranch in New Mexico. Bolson tortoises, some weighing more than 100 pounds, once grazed parts of the southwestern U.S. before disappearing around 10,000 years ago, victims of human hunting. This endangered tortoise now clings to survival, restricted to a single small area in central Mexico. Thus, the reintroduction not only repatriates the tortoise to the U.S., it increases the species's chance for survival. Similar experiments are also occurring outside North America.

"Animals Without Wilderness Are a Closed Book"

If native large carnivores have been killed out of a region, their reintroduction and recovery is the heart of a conservation strategy. Wolves, cougars, lynx, wolverines, grizzly and black bears, jaguars, sea otters, and other top carnivores need to be restored throughout North America in ecologically effective densities in their natural ranges where suitable habitat remains or can be restored. (Obviously, large areas of North America have been so modified by humans and support such large human populations or intensive agriculture that rewilding is not feasible.) Without the goal of rewilding for large areas with large carnivores, we are closing our eyes to what conservation really means—and demands. Disney cinematographer Lois Crisler, after years of filming wolves in the Arctic, wrote, "Wilderness without animals is dead—dead scenery. Animals without wilderness are a closed book."

Dave Foreman,
"Rewilding," Rewilding Institute, *2004.*
http://rewilding.org.

The reintroduction of wild horses and camels would be a logical part of these early experiments. Horses and camels originated on this continent, and many species were present in the late Pleistocene. Today's feral horses and asses that live in some areas throughout the West are plausible substitutes for extinct American species. Because most of the surviving Eurasian and African species are now critically endangered, establishing Asian asses and Przewalski's horse in North America might help prevent the extinction of these animals. Bactrian camels, which are critically endangered in the Gobi Desert, could provide a modern proxy for *Camelops*, a late Pleistocene camel. Camels, introduced from captive or domesticated populations, might benefit U.S. ecosystems by browsing on woody plants that today are overtaking arid grasslands in the Southwest, an ecosystem that is increasingly endangered.

Another prong of the project would likely be more controversial but could also begin immediately. It would establish small numbers of elephants, cheetahs and lions on private property.

Introducing elephants could prove valuable to nearby human populations by attracting tourists and maintaining grasslands useful to ranchers (elephants could suppress the woody plants that threaten southwestern grasslands). In the late Pleistocene, at least four elephant species lived in North America. Under a scientific framework, captive elephants in the U.S. could be introduced as proxies for these extinct animals. The biggest cost involved would be fencing, which has helped reduce conflict between elephants and humans in Africa.

Many cheetahs are already in captivity in the U.S. The greatest challenge would be to provide them with large, securely fenced areas that have appropriate habitat and prey animals. Offsetting these costs are benefits—what must have been strong interactions with pronghorn, facilitating ecotourism as an economic alternative for ranchers, many of whom are struggling financially, and helping to save the world's fastest carnivore from extinction.

Lions are increasingly threatened, with populations in Asia and some parts of Africa critically endangered. Bringing back lions, which are the same species that once lived in North America, presents daunting challenges as well as many potential benefits. But private reserves in southern Africa where lions and other large animals have been successfully reintroduced offer a model—and these reserves are smaller than some private ranches in the Southwest.

If these early experiments with large herbivores and predators show promising results, more could be undertaken, moving toward the long-term goal of a huge ecological history park. What we need now are panels of experts who, for each species, could assess, advise and cautiously lead efforts in restoring megafauna to North America.

A real-world example of how the reintroduction of a top predator might work comes from the wolves of Yellowstone National Park. The gray wolf became extinct in and around Yellowstone during the 1920s. The loss led to increases in their prey—moose and elk—which in turn reduced the distribution of aspens and other trees they eat. Lack of vegetation destroyed habitat for migratory birds and for beavers. Thus, the disappearance of the wolves propagated a trophic cascade from predators to herbivores to plants to birds and beavers. Scientists have started to document the ecosystem changes as reintroduced wolves regain the ecological role they played in Yellowstone for millennia. An additional insight researchers are learning from putting wolves back into Yellowstone is that they may be helping the park cope with climate change. As winters grow milder, fewer elk die, which means less carrion for scavengers such as coyotes, ravens and bald eagles. Wolves provide carcasses throughout the winter for the scavengers to feed on, bestowing a certain degree of stability.

The Challenges Ahead

As our group on the ranch in New Mexico discussed how Pleistocene rewilding might work, we foresaw many challenges that would have to be addressed and overcome. These include the possibility that introduced animals could bring novel diseases with them or that they might be unusually susceptible to diseases already present in the ecosystem; the fact that habitats have changed over the millennia and that reintroduced animals might not fare well in these altered environments; and the likelihood of unanticipated ecological consequences and unexpected reactions from neighboring human communities. Establishing programs that monitor the interactions among species and their consequences for the well-being of the ecosystem will require patience and expertise. And, of course, it will not be easy to convince the public to accept predation as an important natural process that actually nourishes the land and enables ecosystems to thrive. Other colleagues have raised additional concerns, albeit none that seems fatal.

Many people will claim that the concept of Pleistocene rewilding is simply not feasible in the world we live in today. I urge these people to look to Africa for inspiration. The year after the creation of Kruger National Park was announced, the site was hardly the celebrated mainstay of southern African biodiversity it is today. In 1903 zero elephants, nine lions, eight buffalo and very few cheetahs lived within its boundaries. Thanks to the vision and dedication of African conservationists, 7,300 elephants, 2,300 lions, 28,000 buffalo and 250 cheetahs roamed Kruger 100 years later—as did 700,000 tourists, bringing with them tens of millions of dollars.

In the coming century, humanity will decide, by default or design, the extent to which it will tolerate other species and thus how much biodiversity will endure. Pleistocene rewilding is not about trying to go back to the past; it is about using the past to inform society about how to maintain the functional fabric of nature. The potential scientific, conservation and cultural benefits of restoring megafauna are clear, as are the costs. Although sound science can help mitigate the potential costs, these ideas will make many uneasy. Yet given the apparent dysfunction of North American ecosystems and Earth's overall state, inaction carries risks as well. In the face of tremendous uncertainty, science and society must weigh the costs and benefits of bold, aggressive actions like Pleistocene rewilding against those of business as usual, which has risks, uncertainties and costs that are often unacknowledged. We have a tendency to think that if we maintain the status quo, things will be fine. All the available information suggests the opposite.

> "Sometimes [killing invasive species] is
> the only way to protect biodiversity. . . .
> The risk is ending up with a world of
> pigeons, rats, and cockroaches."

Eradicating Invasive Species Can Preserve Endangered Ecosystems

Jane Braxton Little

*Writer and photographer Jane Braxton Little explains in this
viewpoint that a major cause of species extinction, especially on
the world's islands, is nonnative animals introduced over the
centuries by humans—cats, dogs, goats, rats, rabbits, snakes, and
pigeons are common examples—that are so successful they over-
run host ecosystems, setting off chain reactions of species disappearance called trophic cascades. Little presents evidence that
controversial eradication programs—killing invasive animals by
trap, poison, and gunshot—are producing dramatic results:
Threatened seabird populations are rebounding and plants
thought to be extinct have reappeared less than a decade after
eradication began. Many animal protection groups vehemently
oppose wiping out one species to save another, she reports, but*

eradication advocates such as Island Conservation counter that human intervention and lethal measures are warranted when predators that thrive worldwide are causing irreversible ecological damage. Jane Braxton Little's articles on natural resources have appeared in Audubon, Utne, *and other national magazines.*

As you read, consider the following questions:

1. How does the extinction of seabirds by nonnative predators trigger a trophic cascade, according to Little?
2. Why are island ecosystems especially vulnerable to ruin by invasive species, according to the author?
3. What results does the author report from Island Conservation's black rat eradication program in California's Channel Islands National Park?

Shaye Wolf is perched atop a wind-whipped volcanic outcrop on a remote Mexican island. Pacific waves are crashing against boulders on the shore 100 feet below her, where elephant seals are bellowing at the surf. Watching from a lower, safer rock, I hold my breath. Wolf pushes one black fleece sleeve above her elbow and stretches a slender arm through the mouth of a tiny crevice. Reaching deeper, she twists her torso this way and that, still balanced on the precipice. Suddenly she beams me a smile as she pulls a Xantus's murrelet egg out from the rocks.

The egg, which is mother-of-pearl gray and slightly smaller than a chicken's, is mottled with pastel blues and small cinnabar spots. Wolf, a seabird scientist, cradles it protectively. In her palm she holds the promise of an endangered species struggling to survive.

Several breeding seasons ago a scientist would have had a better chance of pulling a European rabbit out of this crevice than a murrelet egg. More than 500 of the nonnative mammals were overrunning this Mexican islet, the largest of the three San Benito Islands, 25 miles off the coast of Baja California. They took over murrelet nest caves, evicted other seabirds from their burrows, and decimated the island's endemic plants.

Invasive Species Annihilate Native Flora and Fauna

Ever since humans began sailing the seas, they have introduced species to islands unprepared for the newcomers. Cats, dogs, goats, pigs, rats, and rabbits—all have taken a harsh toll on fragile island ecosystems. Seabirds especially have suffered. Along the Mexican coast and in the Gulf of California, invasive mammals have annihilated murrelets and four other species on 14 islands. Cats alone wiped out about half the population of laysan albatross on Guadalupe Island in 2001. Until recently they were killing more than 1,000 black-vented shearwaters a month on Natividad Island, breeding ground for 95 percent of the world's population.

While the future of these seabird species is anything but assured, a fledgling conservation group offers the best hope in decades. Since 1997, Island Conservation, based in Santa Cruz, California, and Grupo de Ecologia y Conservacion de Islas, its Mexican partner, have eradicated 39 invasive-mammal populations on 25 islands. The results are dramatic. Seabirds are rebounding. Endemic plants thought extinct have reappeared. Scientists hadn't realized the intruders were suppressing native lizard and salamander populations until they began to notice that these species were flourishing, too.

The Island Conservation partners' technique is as straightforward as it is unsavory: Kill the invaders. Their tools are low-tech: leg traps, poison, and sharpshooters. At a time when the planet is losing species at an unparalleled rate, their mission is to prevent extinctions by protecting and restoring biodiversity, says Bernie Tershy, the group's executive director. "No one is into killing rabbits or even rats. We think of it as making birds."

Controlling exotic species is a grim reality, says Graham Chisholm, conservation director of Audubon California. "While no decision to use lethal measures should be taken lightly, killing should be used as a last resort after all measures have failed; sometimes it is the only way to protect biodiversity," he says. "The risk is ending up with a world of pigeons, rats, and cockroaches."

Island Conservation's deep involvement in eradication makes it a magnet for controversy. Tershy has been accused of everything from animal cruelty to playing God. He does not take the criticism lightly but counters it by telling the tale of the albatross. The largest of all seabirds, albatross can live as long as 75 years. They begin breeding at four or five and mate for life, producing one chick a year. Along comes a cat into a laysan albatross colony, killing birds that are completely defenseless against terrestrial predators. When the birds' mates return from the sea and find their partners dead, they are unable to support their chicks alone. More death. Before long an entire albatross colony disappears.

It gets worse. Nonnative species put entire ecosystems at risk, not just seabirds. The disappearance of one species triggers other disappearances in what conservation biologists call trophic cascades, a series of secondary effects. Like salmon, seabirds are a link between oceanic and terrestrial ecosystems, carrying nutrients from the sea. During their nesting months on islands, the birds fertilize terrestrial plants in the course of their normal activities. Insects and beetles feed on the plants before they become food themselves for lizards and spiders. When predators wipe out seabirds, these connections are destroyed. Eventually island ecosystems become biologically sterile.

Islands harbor an exceptional treasury of plant and animal life that includes marine mammals, bizarre reptiles, and a dizzying array of insects. It is this abundance that so amazed Charles Darwin and Alfred Russel Wallace, contributing to their theories of the origins and adaptations of all species. As mankind extends its dominance around the planet, islands are disproportionately affected, especially by introduced species. Humans may have deposited the first nonnatives accidentally—every shipwreck releases rats. But by the 1770s, when Captain James Cook was sailing the Pacific seas, he and others were deliberately putting ashore goats and pigs, cattle and sheep as hedges against supply shortages on future voyages. Fishermen and other island residents brought in cats as pets and to control mice. Rabbits came for sport hunting.

The results have been horrific. The vast majority of all recorded animal extinctions have been species endemic to islands. Island birds represent a staggering 95 percent of all birds snuffed out. More than half of these extinctions globally are the result of introduced species. On San Benito and other Mexican islands, invasive predators have caused 19 of 21 animal extinctions. . . .

Islands Are Especially Vulnerable

Most islands are remote and inaccessible, which frees them of the development pressures that conflict with conservation efforts elsewhere. Because their ecosystems are relatively intact, they offer the chance to preserve not just species but the evolutionary processes that have been occurring on Islands for millions of years.

Wolf, 33, a Santa Cruz doctoral candidate, is part of the Island Conservation cadre. . . . Before descending from the precipice, she measures, records, and carefully returns the murrelet egg to its exact position in the crevice. The adults, which have not started sitting on this egg, have a limited sense of smell and will not notice the brief disturbance when they

The National Aquatic Invasive Species Act Blocks Entry Via Ships' Ballast Water

Every ship operating in waters of the United States must have an Aquatic Invasive Species Management Plan, carry out Best Management Practices (including practices to reduce hull fouling), document ballast operations and management activities, and comply with applicable ballast water treatment requirements.

Ballast Water Requirements

Until the end of 2011, all existing ships entering a U.S. port must conduct ballast water exchange and any other management practices included in regulations unless the safety of the vessel is at stake. Exceptions include vessels operating entirely within the exclusive economic zone and existing vessels that operate entirely within an enclosed aquatic ecosystem.

Beginning in 2012, all vessels entering a U.S. port shall conduct ballast water treatment so that ballast water discharged contains less than 1 living organism that is larger than 50 micrometers in dimension per 10 cubic meters of water and less than 1 living organism that is smaller than 50 micrometers per 10 milliliters of water.

Senator Carl Levin's Web Site,
Summary of the National Aquatic Invasive Species Act of 2007,
March 1, 2007. www.senate.gov/~levin/.

return from the sea to lay another egg, she says. When their chicks are two days old and still unable to fly, they will lure them down from their cliff nests to the sea. The chicks will not return to land until they are adults and ready to lay their own eggs.

Near a cove where three dolphins cavort in the waves, Wolf crosses a colony of Cassin's auklet nests, hopscotching to avoid collapsing the burrows dug into the sandy soil. Before her first visit to San Benito, rabbits had taken over these seabirds' spots, forcing them to build new burrows. The rabbits' predecessors—goats and donkeys—overran the island when they were brought here in the 1930s.

The effects were devastating to the trio of islets, which combined measure 3.7 square miles. Historically the islands supported one of the largest and most diverse populations of breeding seabirds in North America outside of Alaska—more than 2 million birds from 13 different species and subspecies. Three of the local plants, including the San Benito live-forever, were unique globally. By the time Wolf arrived in 2000, live-forevers were nowhere to be seen—the rabbits had gobbled them all up. The flat, open patches of sandy soil below the cliffs were hard-packed by decades of goat and donkey hooves pounding in the auklets' burrows. Rabbits occupied rock caves and burrows alike.

Today Wolf can tally about 35,000 Cassin's auklet nests and more than 300 for Xantus's murrelets, listed as endangered in Mexico and threatened in California. The island also supports healthy populations of black-vented shearwaters and three species of storm-petrels. Even the plant life is reviving. On a hike across the island, Wolf spots a live-forever, a small, delicate succulent sporting a pale yellow blossom. Long lost to the rabbits, it has come back from seeds lying dormant in the ground.

Wolf credits the San Benitos' recovery to Bill Wood, Island Conservation's first employee. Wood, a hunter and trapper who spent most of his life in the eastern Sierra Nevada near Bishop, California, devoted many months over four years to San Benito. His mission was to wipe out the rabbits. He and Freckles, his Jack Russell terrier, would go to work at dawn. Freckles rousted the rabbits; Wood shot them. By 2001 the rabbits were gone from all three islands. The killing bothers Wood, but after decades of hunting bobcats for their pelts, he says he has a debt to repay. "I saw the damage the rabbits were doing and the benefits to the islands after we were through. I felt I had taken from the resources. This was a way to pay back with something good."

The effects show not just on West San Benito, where Wolf is gathering most of her dissertation data, but also on East San Benito. On a grey afternoon we ride a 20-foot boat through rolling swells to survey seabirds on this foreboding islet, where the Mexican government has banned humans. We float over a deep-green kelp forest and past a colony of California sea lions hauled out on the rocks. Around a bend in a quiet cove, dozens of Guadalupe fur seals lounge on the shore, the only breeding population in the world other than on nearby Guadalupe Island. A yellow-crowned night heron watches us watch the seals.

Wolf starts her census on a steep slope mottled yellow with San Benito tarweed and green with Pacific mallow. While she is counting—46 Brandt's cormorant nests and 195 brown pelican nests—endangered pelicans are feeding around our boat in spectacular plunge dives. Sociable at mealtime, they are sensitive nesters. All it takes, Wolf says, is flushing one brown pelican and that nest is often finished for the year. . . .

Survival Depends on Human Intervention

Most species would fare better without any human contact, but the world has evolved beyond that. Today species' survival depends on the education and responsibility of local communities, says Alfonso Aguirre, director of Island Conservation's Mexican partner, based in Ensenada, Baja Mexico. Once an island is rid of its nonnative invaders, local residents must keep it predator free. "Today there is no nature without people," he says. "The conservation of natural resources is very much connected to the well-being of the community."

Island Conservation's most controversial eradication project was in southern California's Channel Islands National Park, where black rats were overrunning the three islets that comprise Anacapa Island, one of only two regular nesting areas in the United States for Xantus's murrelets. The rats' taste for murrelet eggs had reduced the population to as few as 31 breeding pairs from one that numbered in the hundreds, maybe the thousands. In 2001 and 2002 the Park Service used helicopters to drop poison on Anacapa, including its inaccessible cliffs. Island Conservation organized and conducted the eradication, which National Audubon supported.

The project drew furious opposition from animal-rights activists, who sued to stall the poisoning and waged a publicity campaign citing the "slow, cruel deaths" inflicted on the rats. They challenged the scientific basis for the program, and still remain livid. "It is hubris in the extreme to wipe out one species in favor of another one," says Scarlet Newton of the Channel Islands Animal Protection Association.

For Kate Faulkner, chief of natural resources for Channel Islands National Park, the survival of a species easily justifies the loss of individuals in a species found worldwide. Conserving biological diversity is the Park Service's mission, she says. "I'm not willing to lose the Xantus's murrelet. If Congress wants these islands for a rat sanctuary, they should not be part of a national park."

The poison project was an enormous success for the Anacapa ecosystem. The next breeding season Faulkner found Xantus's murrelets nesting in places where they had never before bred successfully, and some in places where they had not been seen since the 1920s. Nest predation has decreased from nearly 100 percent to less than 20 percent today, and the number of active nests has increased by 80 percent. Faulkner has also found a Cassin's auklet nest, the first ever documented on Anacapa. Native deer mice have rebounded beyond scientists' expectations and are beginning to colonize areas where none were found before the project. The survival rate of juvenile side-blotched lizards has increased; scientists hadn't even realized the rats were suppressing them.

These successes have helped convince the Mexican government to protect seabird habitat. All 20 islands off the Baja coast were recently proposed as a biosphere reserve, which would protect them from development, support small-scale sustainable fishing, and halt habitat destruction.

"*[A]ssisted migration may indeed turn out to be the only way to save some species.*"

Assisted Migration May Be Necessary to Save Endangered Species

Carl Zimmer

Science writer and lecturer Carl Zimmer says the realities of global warming have forced conservationists to seriously consider radical, last-ditch strategies to save endangered species. In this viewpoint, Zimmer makes the case for perhaps the most radical response: Physically picking up a species and moving it "hundreds of miles to a cooler place." Human intervention may be necessary, he says, because climate change is happening too rapidly for species to get out of the way and because human development has put too many obstacles in the way of natural species migration. Zimmer acknowledges that assisted migration involves big problems as well. For example, species are interdependent, so entire networks of species may have to be moved, and no one knows where to draw the line, or whether transplanted species will wreak havoc on ecosystems in which they are essentially invasive. What is certain, he says, is that mass extinction is inevitable in this century if species stay where they are. Carl Zimmer is the author of Evolution: The Triumph of an Idea, *publisher of the science Web blog* The Loom, *and a frequent guest on the National Public Radio programs* Fresh Air *and* This American Life.

As you read, consider the following questions:

1. How will climate change drive the Bay checkerspot butterfly to extinction, according to Zimmer?
2. What evidence does the author give to show that species are already trying to "get out of the way" of global warming?
3. Which species does Zimmer suggest may be impossible to relocate?

The Bay checkerspot butterfly's story is all too familiar. It was once a common sight in the San Francisco Bay area, but development and invasive plants have wiped out much of its grassland habitat. Conservationists have tried to save the butterfly by saving the remaining patches where it survives. But thanks to global warming, that may not be good enough.

Climate scientists expect that the planet will become warmer in the next century if humans continue to produce greenhouse gases like carbon dioxide. The California Climate Change Center projects the state's average temperature will rise 2.6 to 10.8 degrees Fahrenheit. Warming is also expected to cause bigger swings in rainfall.

Studies on the Bay checkerspot butterfly suggest that this climate change will push the insect to extinction. The plants it depends on for food will shift their growing seasons, so that when the butterfly eggs hatch, the caterpillars have little to eat. Many other species may face a similar threat, and conservation biologists are beginning to confront the question of how to respond. The solution they prefer would be to halt global warming. But they know they may need to prepare for the worst.

One of the most radical strategies they are considering is known as assisted migration. Biologists would pick a species up and move it hundreds of miles to a cooler place.

Assisted migration triggers strong, mixed feelings from conservation biologists. They recognize that such a procedure would be plagued by uncertainties and risk. And yet it may be the only way to save some of the world's biodiversity.

"Some days I think this is absolutely, positively something that has to be done," said Dr. Jessica Hellmann of the University of Notre Dame. "And other days I think it's a terrible idea."

Conservation biologists are talking seriously about assisted migration because the effects of climate change are already becoming clear. The average temperature of the planet is 1.6 degrees Fahrenheit higher than it was in 1880. Dr. Camille Parmesan, a biologist at the University of Texas, reviewed hundreds of studies on the ecological effects of climate change this month in the journal *Annual Review of Ecology, Evolution, and Systematics*. Many plant species are now budding earlier in the spring. Animals migrate earlier as well. And the ranges of many species are shifting to higher latitudes, as they track the climate that suits them best.

This is hardly the first time that species have moved in response to climate change. For over two million years, the planet has swung between ice ages and warm periods, causing some species to shift their ranges hundreds of miles. But the current bout of warming may be different. The earth was already relatively warm when it began. "These species haven't seen an earth as warm as this one's going to be in a long, long time," said Dr. Mark Schwartz, a conservation biologist at the University of California, Davis.

Assisted Migration: Last-Ditch Preservation

A dying race is making its last stand in the drippy forests of Florida. Its name is *Torreya taxifolia*, a species of yew tree. Only a few hundred of its kind remain—in some cases, nothing but a few green sprouts pleading for life on a rotting stump. But the tree's quiet demise far away in the woods is causing lots of hubbub.

Torreya is a charismatic tree. Its needled branches have touched the heart of many a naturalist. And so a loose band of enthusiasts calling themselves the Torreya Guardians is now doing exactly what we're scolded not to do in this post-kudzu, exotic-wary age. They're spreading *Torreya* around.

Like a church smuggling refugees to safe houses, they're planting *Torreya* seeds in spots from North Carolina to New York State—up to 1,000 kilometers north of its current geographic range. The Torreya Guardians hope to stem their tree's decline—which they blame on global warming—by moving it north to cooler climes. . . .

Douglas Fox, *"When Worlds Collide,"*
Conservation, *vol. 8, no. 1,*
January–March 2007. www.conbio.org.

It's also going to be more difficult for some species to move, Dr. Schwartz added. When the planet warmed at the end of past ice ages, retreating glaciers left behind empty landscapes. Today's species will face an obstacle course made of cities, farms and other human settlements.

Animals and plants will also have to move quickly. If a species cannot keep up with the shifting climate, its range will shrink. Species that are already limited to small ranges may not be able to survive the loss.

In 2004, an international team of scientists estimated that 15 percent to 37 percent of species would become extinct by 2050 because of global warming. "We need to limit climate change or we wind up with a lot of species in trouble, possibly extinct," said Dr. Lee Hannah, a co-author of the paper and chief climate change biologist at the Center for Applied Biodiversity Science at Conservation International.

Some scientists have questioned that study's methods. Dr. Schwartz calls it an overestimate. Nevertheless, Dr. Schwartz said that more conservative estimates would still represent "a serious extinction."

Many conservation biologists believe that conventional strategies may help combat extinctions from global warming. Bigger preserves, and corridors connecting them, could give species more room to move.

Conservation biologists have also been talking informally about assisted migration. The idea builds on past efforts to save endangered species by moving them to parts of their former ranges. The gray wolf, for example, has been translocated from Canada to parts of the western United States with great success.

When Dr. Jason McLachlan, a Notre Dame biologist, gives talks on global warming and extinction, "someone will say, 'It's not a problem, since we can just FedEx them to anywhere they need to go,'" he said.

No government or conservation group has yet begun an assisted migration for global warming. But discussions have started. "We're thinking about these issues," said Dr. Patrick Gonzalez, a climate scientist at the Nature Conservancy.

The conservancy is exploring many different ways to combat extinctions from global warming, and Dr. Gonzalez says that assisted migration "could certainly be one of the options." For now, the conservancy has no official policy on assisted migration.

As Dr. McLachlan began hearing about assisted migration more often, he became concerned that conservation biologists were not weighing it scientifically. He joined with Dr. Schwartz and Dr. Hellmann to lay out the terms of the debate in a paper to be published in the journal *Conservation Biology*.

Dr. McLachlan and his colleagues argue that assisted migration may indeed turn out to be the only way to save some species. But biologists need to answer many questions before they can do it safely and effectively.

The first question would be which species to move. If tens of thousands are facing extinction, it will probably be impossible to save them all. Conservation biologists will have to make the painful decision about which species to try to save. Some species threatened by climate change, including polar bears and other animals adapted to very cold climates, may have nowhere to go.

The next challenge will be to decide where to take those species. Conservation biologists will have to identify regions where species can survive in a warmer climate. But to make that prediction, scientists need to know how climate controls the range of species today. In many countries, including the United States, that information is lacking.

"We don't even know where species are now," Dr. McLachlan said.

Simply moving a species is no guarantee it will be saved, of course. Many species depend intimately on other species for their survival. If conservation biologists move the Bay checkerspot butterfly hundreds of miles north to Washington, for example, it may not be able to feed on the plants there. Conservation biologists may have to move entire networks of species, and it may be hard to know where to draw the line.

Assisted migration is plagued only with uncertain prospects of success, but potential risks as well. A transplanted species would, in essence, be an invasive one. And it might thrive so well that it would start to harm other species. Invasive species are among the biggest threats to biodiversity in some parts of the world. Many were accidentally introduced but some were intentionally moved with great confidence that they would do no harm. Cane toads were introduced in Australia to destroy pests on sugar plantations, and they proceeded to wipe out much of the continent's wildlife.

"If you're trying to protect a community of species, you're not going to want someone to introduce some tree from Florida," Dr. Hellmann said. "But if you're someone watching that tree go extinct, you're going to want to do it."

Dr. Hellmann and her colleagues do not endorse or condemn assisted migration in their new paper. Instead, they call for other conservation biologists to join in a debate. They hope to organize a meeting this summer to have experts share their ideas.

"There really needs to be a clear conversation about this, so that we can lay all the chips on the table," Dr. Schwartz said.

Other experts on global warming and extinctions praised the new paper for framing the assisted migration debate. "It's certainly on everybody's mind, and people are discussing it quite a lot," Dr. Hannah said. "This paper's a breakthrough in that sense."

Dr. Hannah for one is leery of moving species around. "I'm not a huge fan of assisted migration, but there's no question we'll have to get into it to some degree," he said. "We want to see it as a measure of last resort, and get into it as little as possible."

It is possible that conservation biologists may reject assisted migration in favor of other strategies, Dr. McLachlan said. But the hard questions it raises will not go away. As species shift their ranges, some of them will push into preserves that are refuges for endangered species.

"Even if we don't move anything, they're going to be moving," Dr. McLachlan said. "Do we eradicate them? All of these issues are still relevant."

> *"The ultimate desire is that if we keep tissue samples, we can one day implant these into surrogate parents and get them back."*

Freezing and Storing DNA Could Make Extinction Reversible

Ian Sample

Scientists at the Natural History Museum in London have developed an innovative response to species decline, journalist Ian Sample reports in the following viewpoint. Their project, called the Frozen Ark, involves collecting DNA and tissue samples from endangered species and then freezing and storing the cells in the hope that one day advanced cloning techniques will enable scientists to resurrect species that have gone extinct. Technology cannot achieve this end yet, but Sample argues that as optimism for saving species from extinction by other measures fades, and estimates of how many species will soon be wiped out grow, the Frozen Ark project is a far better alternative than doing nothing, thereby guaranteeing that extinct species will be lost forever. Ian Sample is a science correspondent for the British newspaper Guardian.

Ian Sample, "Frozen Ark to Save Rare Species," www.guardian.co.uk, July 27, 2004. Reproduced by permission of Guardian News Service, LTD.

As you read, consider the following questions:

1. How will stored DNA be useful to scientists even if they can't use it to clone new organisms, according to Sample?

2. How is the Frozen Ark designed to compile and share data on endangered species worldwide, and what precaution helps ensure that frozen samples are not damaged or lost, as described by the author?

3. Which animals went into the "ark" first, according to Sample?

A modern version of Noah's Ark, designed to save thousands of creatures from extinction, was launched yesterday by scientists at the Natural History Museum.

The extraordinary project was set up to protect a vast array of animals, not from epic floods, but from the threat of imminent extinction thanks to humankind's actions. Thousands of species are expected to be wiped out within the next few decades because of pollution, war and the destruction of natural habitats.

Rather than being offered refuge on a giant wooden boat, the threatened species face a more prosaic salvation at the bottom of a deep-freeze unit in one of the museum's laboratories in west London.

While entire colonies of some creatures will be frozen, in most cases only DNA and tissue samples of endangered species will be stored.

Scientists behind the project, dubbed the Frozen Ark, are keen to preserve the DNA of endangered animals so they can continue research into their evolutionary histories even if they become extinct. More ambitiously, scientists hope one day to be able to use cells from the frozen tissue samples to recreate extinct animals using advanced cloning techniques.

The World's Zoos Are High-Tech Arks

For some at-risk species, biotech conservation represents the last chance to preserve precious genetic diversity, a benchmark of species health and well-being. Toward this end, zoos have become genetic repositories for cryogenically frozen eggs, embryos, sperm and tissue.

The first so-called "frozen zoo" was created in 1975 by Kurt Benirschke, a visionary physician who switched from his human practice to work with endangered species at the San Diego Zoo, studying gene pools and genetic diseases made prevalent by inbreeding.

Today, in zoos around the world, these deep-freeze tanks act as a high-tech Ark, housing cells from the planet's most endangered animals, including chimps, cheetahs, pandas, California condors and hundreds more.

As a result, long-dead animals are now becoming parents from the grave, with their precious DNA still circulating in the gene pool.

Sharon Guynup,
"Biotech the Latest Defense in Animal-Extinction Fight,"
National Geographic Today, *January 16, 2003.*
http://news.nationalgeographic.com.

"Because of man's actions, species are going extinct at an alarming rate. We're losing them now at a rate that's as serious as the great extinctions," said Philip Rainbow, of the Natural History Museum.

"The ultimate desire is that if we keep tissue samples, we can one day implant these into surrogate parents and get them back. It may sound fanciful, but it'd be a great pity if in 40 years' time scientists are saying, 'look what we can do now, why didn't you keep tissue samples of these animals?'"

Yesterday, DNA samples from the scimitar-horned oryx, which was declared extinct in the wild last year, became the first to be deposited, along with samples from the Socorro dove, a coral fish called the banggai cardinal, the yellow seahorse and the mountain chicken, which is actually a variety of Caribbean frog.

Other species will follow shortly, including the Polynesian tree snail, the Fregate island beetle, which is considered critically endangered, and the British field cricket, of which fewer than 100 remain in the wild. In the next 30 years, scientists predict 1,130 species of mammals and 1,183 species of birds will die out.

Not all the samples will be stored at the Natural History Museum. Part of the project will involve the creation of a database that holds worldwide information on DNA and tissue samples. As an insurance against damage or loss of the frozen samples, duplicates will be kept in chosen institutions around the world.

Tentative attempts to use cloning to bring back extinct species are already under way. Scientists at the Australian Museum in Sydney are painstakingly trying to piece together fragments of Tasmanian tiger DNA from pickled pups in the hope of resurrecting the animal, which was hunted to extinction more than 60 years ago.

Even if they are successful, they face another hurdle in identifying a suitable species to carry a cloned egg of the extinct animal without rejecting it.

Last year, scientists in Japan announced ambitious plans to attempt to clone prehistoric woolly mammoths after extracting DNA samples from mammoths dug from the Russian permafrost. Their chances of success also rely largely on whether the DNA is in good enough condition, which many scientists think unlikely.

According to Prof Rainbow, the Frozen Ark is possibly the best chance of being able to ensure that even if certain species are wiped out in the coming decades, they may not be lost for ever.

"It may sound depressing that we feel we have to do this, but it would be even worse if we did nothing," he said.

"We're not trying to play Frankenstein, we're just trying to preserve biological tissues in such a way that somebody someday might be able to do something useful with it. Fifty years ago we couldn't imagine doing the kinds of things we can do now."

Two by Two: Who's First in Noah's New Zoo

The scimitar-horned oryx. Named after its scimitar-shaped horns, the oryx (Oryx dammah) used to range throughout northern Africa. Overhunting, desertification and continuing wars in Africa have all contributed to its demise. Declared extinct in the wild in 2003, it exists now only in specialised breeding programmes in captivity.

The Socorro dove. Unique to Socorro, a remote island off the west coast of Mexico, the Socorro dove (Zenaida graysoni) has been in terminal decline since 1957 due to habit loss and latterly the introduction of domestic cats. The birds are now being bred in captivity and plans are in place to reintroduce them to the wild if their habitat can be made safe.

The mountain chicken. Curiously, not a chicken at all, but a Caribbean frog surviving only on the islands of Montserrat and Dominica. The remaining mountain chicken (Leptodactylus fallax) population was hit badly by the Montserrat volcano eruption. On Dominica, it suffered from being a national dish, a misfortune compounded by a devastating skin fungus epidemic. Now being bred in captivity.

The banggai cardinal. Measuring just a few centimetres long, the banggai cardinal (Pterapogon kauderni) is a black and white fish living on coral reefs. The species is only found in a small region of reefs and is now threatened by over-collection by the pet trade.

The yellow seahorse. Endangered thanks to its appeal to aquarium owners and its use in Chinese medicine, the yellow seahorse (Hippocampus kuda) is now being bred in captivity in the hope of restoring its numbers in the wild. They have chameleon-like eyes that can swivel independently. Females lay their eggs in pouches on the male's belly, and the male later gives birth to live young.

Periodical Bibliography

The following articles have been selected to supplement the diverse views presented in this chapter.

Dana Blanton — "Jobs More Important than Endangered Species," *FOX News*, June 14, 2007.

Richard Buchholz — "Conservation Biology: An Effective and Relevant Conservation Tool," *Trends in Ecology & Evolution*, August 2007.

Jeremy Caplan — "Rare Trees for Sale," *Time*, November 6, 2006.

Jordi Lopez-Pujol, et al. — "Can the Preservation of Historical Relics Permit the Conservation of Endangered Plant Species?" *Conservation Genetics*, August 2007.

Emily Masamitsu — "Re-Engineering the Planet: As the War on Global Warming Heats Up, Some Scientists Argue That Meddling with the Environment Might Be the Only Way to Save It," *Popular Mechanics*, June 2007.

Elizabeth McGowan — "Water Wins Over Wildlife," *Waste News*, July 9, 2007.

Jason S. McLachlan, Jessica J. Hellman, and Mark W. Schwartz — "A Framework for Debate of Assisted Migration in an Era of Climate Change," *Conservation Biology*, April 2007.

New Orleans CityBusiness — "Audubon Nature Institute Hatches World's First 'Cyrochick,'" August 2, 2007.

New York Times Upfront — "Frogs Airlifted to Safety," October 9, 2006.

D. H. Reed, A. C. Nicholas, and G. E. Stratton — "Genetic Quality of Individuals Impacts Population Dynamics," *Animal Conservation*, August 2007.

C. Tisdell, C. Wilson, and H. Swarna Nantha — "Public Choice of Species for the 'Ark,'" *Journal for Nature Conservation*, vol. 54, no. 2, 2006.

For Further Discussion

Chapter 1

1. Julia Whitty estimates that 40 percent of the examined species on Earth are at risk of extinction. In contrast, the *Environment News Service* reports that conservation efforts have successfully put hundreds of endangered species on the road to recovery and suggests that many, such as the bald eagle, are now healthy. Both authors reach their conclusions by extrapolating from a small set of data. Which steps in their calculations involve uncertainty? How might this uncertainty affect the accuracy of their estimates?

2. The Millennium Ecosystem Assessment warns that biodiversity loss means decreases in worldwide food production. Martin Jenkins maintains that enough unused suitable cropland exists in South America and sub-Saharan Africa to yield a net increase in food production despite biodiversity loss. Based on evidence in these viewpoints, do you believe there are inevitable limits to increasing food production? If so, what are they?

Chapter 2

1. Researchers refer to the time delay between present-day temperature increase and future species extinction as "extinction debt." The *World Climate Report* suggests there is likewise a time delay between present-day temperature increase and future species *increase* called "colonization lags." In your opinion, will today's climate change cause more future extinctions than colonizations, or vice versa? Use evidence from the IPCC and *World Climate Report* viewpoints to support your answer.

2. How does the debate over the threat of invasive species depend on the definition of "invasive," and how do Rhett Butler's and Dana Joel Gattuso's definitions differ?

Chapter 3

1. The Union of Concerned Scientists calls the Endangered Species Act (ESA) a success because less than one percent of listed species have gone extinct since the act took effect in 1973. Peyton Knight calls the act a failure because less than 1 percent of listed species have recovered since 1973. Is either statistic a good measure of the act's effectiveness, in your view? If so, why? If not, how should the effectiveness of the ESA be measured? Use evidence from the viewpoints to support your answers.

2. D. Noah Greenwald and Kieran F. Suckling say species are languishing and dying because official foot dragging delays their listing under the Endangered Species Act. But Franck Courchamp et al. urge legislators *not* to list a species as endangered unless it can be fully protected, because certifying its rarity makes it more valuable, more sought after in the wild, and ultimately more endangered. What would it take to "fully protect" endangered species from determined poachers, traders, and collectors, in your opinion? Can such measures be employed without effectively placing these species in captivity?

Chapter 4

1. C. Josh Donlan uses a high-profile example, the reintroduction of gray wolves to Yellowstone National Park, to support his argument that Asian and African predator species can and should coexist with humans in North America. Do his arguments make sense to you? What are some problems that could arise that Donlan does not address in his proposal?

2. Jane Braxton Little, Carl Zimmer, and Ian Sample justify human intervention in species migration and extinction in the interests of biodiversity and human survival. In your opinion, are human interventions such as selective species eradication, assisted migration, and cloning of extinct species likely to preserve biodiversity or invite unintended consequences and cause more problems? To what degree should humans attempt to influence or control "natural" biological and environmental processes?

Organizations to Contact

The editors have compiled the following list of organizations concerned with the issues debated in this book. The descriptions are derived from materials provided by the organizations. All have publications or information available for interested readers. The list was compiled on the date of publication of the present volume; the information provided here may change. Be aware that many organizations take several weeks or longer to respond to inquiries, so allow as much time as possible.

African Wildlife Foundation (AWF)
1400 16th St. NW, Suite 120, Washington, DC   20036
(202) 939-3333 • fax: (202) 939-3332
e-mail: africanwildlife@awf.org
Web site: www.awf.org

The African Wildlife Foundation (AWF), founded in 1961, works to conserve Africa's endangered species (public awareness campaigns focus on large mammals) through the design and implementation of parks, preserves, and projects such as the African Heartland Program, International Gorilla Conservation Program, Mweka College of African Wildlife Management, and the Kenyan eco-lodge Sanctuary at OI Lentille. The Foundation publishes three e-newsletters on its activities in Kenya, Tanzania, and Zambezi; its Web site offers an educational wildlife photo gallery, interactive maps, and news articles.

Convention on International Trade in Endangered Species of Wild Fauna and Flora (CITES)
International Environment House, Chemin des Anémones,
   CH-1219 Chatelaine, Geneva
   Switzerland
(+41) 22-917-8139 • fax: (+41) 22-797-3417

e-mail: info@cites.org
Web site: www.cites.org

The Convention on International Trade in Endangered Species of Wild Fauna and Flora (CITES) is an international agreement between governments, currently of 172 countries, committed to ensure that the international trade in specimens of wild animals and plants does not threaten their survival. Since the convention took force in 1975, all import and export of covered species must be authorized through a licensing system; covered species are listed on one of three Appendices according to the degree of protection they need. The CITES managing authority in the United States is the U.S. Fish and Wildlife Service in Washington, D.C. Available on the CITES Web site are the full Appendices and the latest listing and delisting decisions, export quotas and guidelines for transport, national reports, and a wide variety of publications including the e-book for laypersons *The Evolution of CITES* and the bi-annual newsletter *CITES World*.

George C. Marshall Institute
1625 K St. NW, Suite 1050, Washington, DC   20006
(202) 296-9655 • fax: (202) 296-9714
e-mail: info@marshall.org
Web site: www.marshall.org

The George C. Marshall Institute, a nonprofit organization founded in 1984, takes a skeptical minority position on global warming science. It argues that the scientific view of the causes and effects of global climate change, including the contribution of human activity and the danger to animal and plant species, is unproven and politicized. ExxonMobil, a major funder of the Institute in its early years, has since distanced itself in the face of growing evidence that refutes its positions. Other petroleum producers continue to fund the Institute's programs. The Institute publishes reports opposing premature restrictions on greenhouse gas emissions and regular *George C. Marshall Institute Studies* and *Washington Roundtables on Science and Public Policy*.

International Fund for Animal Welfare (IFAW)
411 Main St., PO Box 193, Yarmouth Port, MA   02675
(508) 744-2000 • fax: (508) 744-2009
e-mail: info@ifaw.org
Web site: www.ifaw.org

The International Fund for Animal Welfare (IFAW) is a nonprofit animal advocacy organization founded in the 1970s to combat Canadian commercial white-coat harp seal hunting. Today it campaigns to protect animals all over the world that are domesticated as well as endangered, in captivity or in the wild. Its informative Web site offers statistics and detailed description of dozens of targeted species and their habitats. The fund publishes annual reports, animal campaign fact sheets, position papers, and the quarterly *IFAW Newsletter.*

International Panel on Climate Change (IPCC)
IPCC Secretariat, c/o World Meteorological Organization, 7bis
   Avenue de la Paix, C.P. 2300, Geneva 2   CH-1211
   Switzerland
(+41) 22-730-8208 • fax: (+41) 22-730-8025
e-mail: IPCC-Sec@wmo.int
Web site: www.ipcc.ch

The International Panel on Climate Change (IPCC), established by the World Meteorological Organization (WMO) and the United Nations Environment Programme (UNEP) in 1988, evaluates global climate change and the role of human activity in global warming, based on accumulated, international, scientific evidence and peer-reviewed, published findings. Its reports are widely cited as authoritative assessments of the current status and likely effects of climate change. The *IPCC Fourth Assessment Report* (known as AR4), issued in 2007 and available in summary and full forms on the official Web site, is an urgent call to action. It concludes that global warming is unequivocal, that it is due to greenhouse gas emissions caused by human activity (with greater than 90 percent confidence), that atmospheric concentrations of carbon dioxide, nitrous oxide, and methane are far higher than they have been for

650,000 years, and that a "business as usual" response will lead to catastrophic species extinction. In addition to the AR4, the IPCC publishes technical papers, methodology reports, press releases and speeches, graphs, and a calendar of expert meetings and workshops.

National Endangered Species Act Reform Coalition (NESARC)

1050 Thomas Jefferson St., 7th Floor, Washington, DC   20007
(202) 333-7481 • fax: (202) 338-2416
e-mail: nesarc@vnf.com
Web site: www.nesarc.org

The National Endangered Species Act Reform Coalition (NESARC), a coalition of roughly 150 member organizations including rural irrigators, municipalities, farm bureaus, electric utilities, forestry companies, builders associations, and property owners, seeks legislative reform of overly restrictive, vague, and inflexible standards and requirements of the Endangered Species Act (ESA) and litigates ESA disputes. NESARC calls for fair compensation and a greater decision-making role for property owners whose property use and value is reduced by ESA restrictions, cost-effective recovery plans, and more stringent scientific evidence that ESA actions are warranted. The coalition issues biweekly updates and analysis of new regulations, white papers, legal briefs, and congressional hearing transcripts.

National Wildlife Federation (NWF)

11100 Wildlife Center Dr., Reston, VA   20190-5362
(800) 822-9919
Web site: www.nwf.org

The National Wildlife Federation (NWF) is a nonprofit grassroots organization dedicated to habitat and wildlife conservation in the United States. Several of its activities are geared for young people, including its magazines *National Wildlife, Ranger Rick, Your Big Backyard,* and *Wild Animal Baby;* its blogs *Green*

Hour and *Wildlife Promise*; and its annual Connie Awards, recognizing individual effort in restoring wildlife habitat and conserving American wildlife.

The Nature Conservancy
4245 N. Fairfax Dr., Suite 100, Arlington, VA   22203-1606
(800) 628-6860
Web site: www.nature.org

The Nature Conservancy is a leading national organization that identifies and preserves ecologically important habitats around the world through the key protection tools of land acquisition and debt-for-nature swaps, by which a portion of a country's foreign debt is forgiven for setting aside conservation land. Founded in 1951, the Conservancy reports roughly a million members and the protection of 17 million acres (69,000 sq.km) in the United States and 117 million acres (473,000 sq.km) internationally. Its publications include the quarterly magazine *Nature Conservancy*, field guides, and the e-newsletter *Great Places*. The Conservancy's Web site describes current projects worldwide and offers numerous "homework help" links to Conservancy resources on issues such as ecotourism, invasive species, rainforests, fire management, and conservation science.

The Rewilding Institute (TRI)
PO Box 13768, Albuquerque, NM   87192
e-mail: TRI@rewilding.org
Web site: www.rewilding.org

The Rewilding Institute (TRI) is a conservation think tank that advocates wildlife conservation on a continental scale. Its primary proposal is the scientifically credible, practically managed introduction of large carnivores such as lions, tigers, bears, and wolves into suitable habitats in North America (sometimes called Pleistocene rewilding) along with the creation of linked migration routes across the continent to allow animals' natural movement. TRI argues that humans and top predators once did and can again coexist in North America, and that without such a radical rewilding plan, dwindling populations of predator species in Africa and Asia are doomed. The Institute's Web site offers abundant links to conservation biology and wilderness area design sites and publications such as environmental activist and TRI founder Dave Foreman's book *Rewilding North America.*

U.S. Fish and Wildlife Service (FWS)

4401 N. Fairfax Dr., Room 420, Arlington, VA   22203
(703) 358-1949 • fax: (703) 358-2271
Web site: www.fws.gov/endangered

The U.S. Fish and Wildlife Service (FWS), a division of the U.S. Department of the Interior, is one of two federal agencies responsible for administering and enforcing the Endangered Species Act and CITES, national listing and delisting of threatened and endangered animal and plant species, and compiling general statistics on the status of protected species. (It shares responsibility with the National Oceanic and Atmospheric Administration Fisheries.) The FWS also issues permits for a range of activities that can potentially impact a species' recovery, such as captive breeding programs and habitat conservation plans, taxidermy, falconry, and the transport of live or dead animals or animal products. (Fishing and hunting licenses are issued by state wildlife agencies, not the FWS.) The Endangered Species Program publishes a wide variety of fact sheets, brochures, handbooks, and periodicals, including the quarterly *Endangered Species Bulletin*, available for free download at the service's Web site.

The Wildlands Project

PO Box 5284, Titusville, FL   32783
(877) 554-5234 • fax: (877) 554-5234
e-mail: info@wildlandsproject.org
Web site: www.twp.org

Cofounded by conservation biologist Michael Soulé and fellow wilderness advocate Dave Foreman in 1991, the nonprofit, nonpartisan Wildlands Project maintains that habitat fragmentation caused by human development is causing critical biodiversity loss. Its mission is the restoration of endangered North American species and habitats, based on public- and private-sector cooperation in establishing a vast network of connected wilderness areas, called MegaLinkages, that allow species to roam freely and safely across the continent from Mexico to the Yukon, Florida to Newfoundland, and Baja California to the Bering Sea. The project has completed six smaller Wildlife Network Designs (WNDs) linking wildlands in the Sky Islands, New Mexico Highlands, Heart of the West, Southern Rockies, Northern Appalachians, and Grand Canyon, and offers these designs to communities and conservation groups as blueprints for protecting key lands. Detailed information on each WND is available on the project's Web site, along with articles and an e-newsletter.

World Conservation Union (IUCN)

1630 Connecticut Ave. NW, 3rd Floor
Washington, DC   20009-1053
(202) 387-4826 • fax: (202) 387-4823
e-mail: postmaster@iucnus.org
Web site: www.iucn.org

Widely known by the name it held from 1956 to 1990—the International Union for the Conservation of Nature and Natural Resources (IUCN)—the World Conservation Union is an important network of hundreds of governmental and nongovernmental agencies and thousands of scientists from 181 countries dedicated to preservation of biodiversity and ecologically sustainable use of natural resources. The union sponsors scientific research and congresses; coordinates resource management projects such as the global Water and Nature Initiative and Peace Parks; and investigates emergencies such as the 2007 killing of critically endangered mountain gorillas in the Democratic Republic of Congo. Its primary publication is the annual *IUCN Red List*, the world's most authoritative inventory of endangered animal and plant species. The IUCN Web site offers an up-to-date news section; its publications catalog lists over 3000 documents, more than 600 of which are free and downloadable.

World Wildlife Fund (WWF)
1250 24th St. NW, PO Box 97180
Washington, DC   20090-7180
(202) 293-4800
e-mail: membership@wwfus.org
Web site: www.worldwildlife.org

The World Wildlife Fund (WWF), a charity founded in 1961, is the world's largest independent conservation organization, with 5 million supporters in more than ninety countries. It sponsors and runs more than a thousand field projects worldwide in the effort to halt and reverse the destruction of biodiversity and natural habitat. WWF work focuses on three biomes—forests, freshwater ecosystems, and oceans and coasts—and eight flagship species—giant pandas, tigers, whales, dolphins, rhinos, elephants, marine turtles, and great apes. The WWF publishes books on endangered wildlife, wild places, and global environmental challenges and the bimonthly newsletter *Focus*. A full bibliography of its conservation science articles, with abstracts, is available on its Web site, as are interactive maps, photo galleries, and links to current campaign sites.

Bibliography of Books

Books

Yvonne Baskin — *A Plague of Rats and Rubbervines: The Growing Threat of Species Invasions*. Washington, DC: Island, 2003.

Michael Boulter — *Extinction: Evolution and the End of Man*. New York: Columbia University Press, 2002.

Bonnie B. Burgess — *Fate of the Wild: The Endangered Species Act and the Future of Biodiversity*. Athens: University of Georgia Press, 2003.

Marla Cone — *Silent Snow: The Slow Poisoning of the Arctic*. New York: Grove, 2005.

Kirsten Dow and Thomas E. Downing — *The Atlas of Climate Change: Mapping the World's Greatest Challenge*. Berkeley: University of California Press, 2006.

Richard Ellis — *The Empty Ocean: Plundering the World's Marine Life*. Washington, DC: Island, 2003.

Richard Ellis — *No Turning Back: The Life and Death of Animal Species*. New York: HarperCollins, 2004.

Linda K. Glover and Sylvia A. Earle, eds. — *Defying Ocean's End: An Agenda for Action*. Washington, DC: Island, 2004.

Dale D. Goble, J. Michael Scott, and Frank W. Davis, eds.

The Endangered Species Act at Thirty: Renewing the Conservation Promise. Washington, DC: Island, 2005.

Al Gore

An Inconvenient Truth: The Planetary Emergency of Global Warming and What We Can Do About It. Emmaus, PA: Rodale, 2006.

Peter Heller

The Whale Warriors: The Battle at the Bottom of the World to Save the Planet's Largest Mammals. New York: Free Press, 2007.

Jodi A. Hilty, William Z. Lidicker Jr., and Adina M. Merenlender

Corridor Ecology: The Science and Practice of Linking Landscapes for Biodiversity Conservation. Washington, DC: Island, 2006.

Sylvan Ramsey Kaufman and Wallace Kaufman

Invasive Plants: A Guide to Identification, Impacts, and Control of Common North American Species. Mechanicsburg, PA: Stackpole, 2007.

Roger Kaye

Last Great Wilderness: The Campaign to Establish the Arctic National Wildlife Refuge. Fairbanks: University of Alaska Press, 2006.

Elizabeth Kolbert

Field Notes from a Catastrophe: Man, Nature, and Climate Change. New York: Bloomsbury, 2006.

Michael Lannoo, ed.

Amphibian Declines: The Conservation Status of United States Species. Berkeley: University of California Press, 2005.

Richard Leakey and Virginia Morell   *Wildlife Wars: My Fight to Save Africa's Natural Treasures.* New York: St. Martin's, 2002.

David B. Lindenmayer and Joern Fischer   *Habitat Fragmentation and Landscape Change: An Ecological and Conservation Synthesis.* Washington, DC: Island, 2006.

Bjorn Lomborg   *Cool It: The Skeptical Environmentalist's Guide to Global Warming.* New York: Knopf, 2007.

Thomas E. Lovejoy and Lee Hannah, eds.   *Climate Change and Biodiversity.* New Haven, CT: Yale University Press, 2005.

David S. Maehr, Reed F. Noss, and Jeffery L. Larkin, eds.   *Large Mammal Restoration: Ecological and Sociological Challenges in the 21st Century.* Washington, DC: Island, 2001.

Paul S. Martin   *Twilight of the Mammoths: Ice Age Extinctions and the Rewilding of America.* Berkeley: University of California Press, 2005.

George C. McGavin   *Endangered: Wildlife on the Brink of Extinction.* Buffalo, NY: Firefly, 2006.

Elliott A. Norse and Larry B. Crowder, eds.   *Marine Conservation Biology: The Science of Maintaining the Sea's Biodiversity.* Washington, DC: Island, 2005.

Susan R. Playfair   *Vanishing Species: Saving the Fish, Sacrificing the Fisherman.* Hanover, NH: University Press of New England, 2005.

Callum M. Roberts — *The Unnatural History of the Sea.* Washington, DC: Island/Shearwater, 2007.

Michael L. Rosenzweig — *Win-Win Ecology: How the Earth's Species Can Survive in the Midst of Human Enterprise.* New York: Oxford University Press, 2003.

James Gustave Speth — *Red Sky at Morning: America and the Crisis of the Global Environment.* New Haven, CT: Yale University Press, 2004.

Peter D. Ward — *Under a Green Sky: Global Warming, the Mass Extinctions of the Past, and What They Can Tell Us About Our Future.* New York: Smithsonian, 2007.

Scott Weidensaul — *The Ghost with Trembling Wings: Science, Wishful Thinking, and the Search for Lost Species.* New York: North Point Press, 2003.

Alan Weisman — *The World Without Us.* New York: Thomas Dunne/St. Martin's, 2007.

Edward O. Wilson — *The Creation: An Appeal to Save Life on Earth.* New York: W. W. Norton, 2007.

Edward O. Wilson — *The Future of Life.* New York: Knopf, 2002.

Index